I'LL OVERCOME, SOMEDAY

from Behind to Ahead of
the Fear Curve

Arun Kumar Misra

AF516844

BlueRose ONE
Stories Matter

© Arun Kumar Misra 2023

All rights reserved

All rights reserved by author. No part of this publication may be reproduced, stored in a retrieval system or transmitted in any form or by any means, electronic, mechanical, photocopying, recording or otherwise, without the prior permission of the author.

Although every precaution has been taken to verify the accuracy of the information contained herein, the author and publisher assume no responsibility for any errors or omissions. No liability is assumed for damages that may result from the use of information contained within.

First Published in January 2023

ISBN: 978-93-5704-632-9

BLUEROSE PUBLISHERS

www.BlueRoseONE.com

info@bluerosepublishers.com

+91 8882 898 898

Cover Design:

Muskan Sachdeva

Typographic Design:

Rohit

Distributed by: BlueRose, Amazon, Flipkart

DEDICATED TO...

*My **Late Pitaji** whose struggles made me learn how to fight against the odds in life, my **Late Amma** who made me learn the importance of family, patience, persistence, and endurance as well as my **Late Wife, Reena** who stood by me always and made me realize that those who genuinely love never go away and walk side by side holding hands together.*

Acknowledgements

Writing a book is harder than I thought and more rewarding than I could have ever imagined.

None of this would have been possible but for Mr. Ankur Mishra, a young author of many prize-winning books, who acted as a source of inspiration to convert my life experiences into a book.

I owe an enormous debt of gratitude to Mrs. Soma Das who gave me constructive suggestions, even before and after I had started penning down my experiences, about the contents of the book. I thank her for keen insight and editorial help.

A very special thanks to Mrs. Shruti Pawagi, the beta reader of my book, for sparing time and making efforts to not just read my draft book, but send detailed comments and feedback.

To my family, my daughter Puja, son-in-law Pankaj and son Shivam for their continuous motivation and encouragement during the period of my writing the book and for always being the family I could turn to during those dark and desperate days. I am always grateful to my little Champ and Grandson Bunny, the greatest gift to my life, for keeping me alive with his witty talks over phone and in person.

I would also like to thank all who contributed to this book in any way, my friends, ex-colleagues & relatives.

Finally, I would like to thank you, the reader, for your interest, time, and trust to read my maiden book.

Message from the Author

"It is really hard to be lonely for very long in a world of words. Even if you do not have friends somewhere, you still have language, and it will find you and wrap its little syllables around you and suddenly there will be a story to live in."- Unknown

Both reading and writing are experiences in which we encounter incidents or facts in our minds with the power of imagination. Before you start experiencing my voyage, let me thank you for choosing my book to spend your precious time with me. In a world where everyone wants to talk about herself/himself, but nobody wants to listen, if you are the one who chose to buy this book and not borrow it, I thank you once again!

Writing about experiences indeed decreases one's sense of isolation. They deepen and widen and expand the sense of life. Creating this book has not helped me overcome my pain altogether but has certainly fed my soul. It gave me a shot at dancing with, or at least clapping along with the absurdity of life instead of being squashed by it. It was like singing on a boat during a terrible storm at sea. You cannot stop the raging storm, but singing can change the hearts and spirits of the people who are together on that ship. Just remember the scene from Titanic Movie- the drowning ship & the musicians.

All the incidents recorded in this book occurred with sprinkling elements of fiction as per taste. Has this book 'happened' to you? If someone asks, my answer to that question will be "yes!" I am unsure how you will take it but as you read this book word by word and page by page, you will participate in its creation. When a novice writer like me makes you shake your head with the exactness of his prose and truths and even makes you laugh about life, he achieves his goal.

I hope reading this book will be an exercise in empathy and walking in my shoes for a while. When I thought my pain and heartbreak were unprecedented in the history of the world, but then I read, went to a think tank, and created this little piece. This book taught me that the things that tormented me most were the very things that connected me with all the people who were alive, who had ever been alive.

Regards,

ARUN KUMAR MISRA

I'LL OVERCOME, SOMEDAY...

..From behind to ahead of the fear curve..

CONTENTS

THE SALAD DAYS

If or not kids inherit the spirit to fight against the odds in life from their parents is a million-dollar question. Though science is silent on this point, I am sure, kids do inherit this spirit from their parents. The art of struggle they wage in life to remain afloat with their heads held high, I believe, comes from parents. It is either the father or mother who just ignites the fire to fight the odds in the lives of their kids. As per prevailing faith and belief, the father is the role model of a kid. However, for me, fortunately or unfortunately, both of my parents have been my role models who gave me lessons of how to carry on the struggle in life not through any lectures or classes but by the way they carried themselves in their lives notwithstanding the adversities they faced and their demeanour on the stage called life. I, as a kid, could hear about the struggles of my father post the sudden and sad demise of his father or watch the struggles of my widowed mother before my eyes post the demise of her husband. Their struggles have impacted our past, continue to impact our present and I am sure, will impact our future as well.

"Struggle teaches us a lot of things,
I am fortunate and unfortunate as well that I
witnessed a roller coaster"

Going ahead, my grandfather left for his heavenly abode at an early age when my father Late Ram Mohan Lal Misra, whom we addressed as Pitaji, was just nine. My Grandfather was survived by my Dadi, whom we called Badi Amma, two daughters, my Buas, and a son, my Pitaji himself. The huge responsibility of taking care of the entire family was thrust upon Pitaji at a tender age when kids generally would go to school and play, unaware of life's brutalities. Being the eldest of the siblings, he endured it for respectful survival not for himself but also for his mother and sisters. He had no idea how to carry on and where to start from. At this point, one of his distant yet closest cousins appeared on the scene and under his umbrella, he moved ahead.

He started the second innings of his life with his widowed mother and two spinster younger sisters.

"When you know why, how becomes easy"

Pitaji knew the WHY of his life and that was to come out of the woods of life come what may. Now, it was the question of HOW. As a normal middle-class boy having bequeathed nothing by his ancestors, he had only one thing and that was his academics. He was a brilliant student and hence could realize that his academic brilliance was the answer to HOW. And that was the only weapon he had, that could take him and his family out of the rough of life facing in their faces, besides God's blessings and lady luck.

He continued his studies and managed to reach the Provincial Civil Service (PCS) interview. But as luck would have it, he could not make it to the list of successful candidates. However, he refused to give in the towel and continued till he got an excellent job in the Audit department of the state government called Local Funds Accounts.

Hailing from a conservative Brahmin family, immediately after getting a job, Pitaji was put under pressure to get married. He, being an obedient son, got married to a girl named Annapurna Tiwari, who later became our mother and whom we addressed as Amma. After a few years, Pitaji disposed of his first responsibility by getting Badi Bua married with a man who was literary and had political links. As luck had not been on the side of my Pitaji, my Fufa (Bua's husband) did not give my Bua the respect a wife deserves, for the reasons best known to him. The hell had broken loose on the Pitaji but, being a man of never say die attitude, he just endured it. My self-respecting Pitaji later brought Bua back home where his son, our Gopal dada was born. The struggling life book of Pitaji now has another difficult chapter to take care of.

Here, started the struggle of Amma. As is known, it is always tough for a newly married lady to live with her sister-in-law discarded by her husband, besides the widowed mother-in-law and one unmarried sister-in-law. Badi Bua would always remain gloomy and worried about her life and her son's future and often do such acts as would vitiate the atmosphere of the house. Though, ideally, everyone could understand that such conduct of Bua was because of the position she was in, practically it would often become irritating for everyone, including Badi Amma, Pitaji, and of course Amma. There is no denying that a married woman, if not given due respect and love by her husband, becomes so irritating that she cannot stand the scene of others being happy.

"Just because you have suffered pain Does not give you the right to Make someone else suffer"

Badi Amma and Pitaji would often act tough with Bua but my Amma had no option but to simply acquiesce to the situation. Fufa would also occasionally call on us only to vitiate the air of the house as it had always ended with unpleasant hot talks. This scenario continued for a couple of years. Amma, however, carried on decently striking a balance to keep the cordiality of relations. Amma had shown that for the sake of family certain things need to be digested even if it antagonizes your liking and attitude. For her, it was Family first.

"We may have our differences, but Nothing is more important than family"

Pitaji, later, got his second sister married as well. Fortunately, my Choti Bua did not face the fate the Badi Bua had, but she too was not as happy in her in-law's house as Pitaji would have expected. My second Fufa's was a huge joint family where internal family disputes were the reason for the disturbing ambience of the house. Moreover, my second Fufa was a very subdued person which led others in the family to dominate him. And, when the husband was not getting due regard in the family, it was unthinkable that the wife would get the due regard. But it was a matter of consolation that Choti Bua did not have to go the Badi Bua's way. In nutshell, it can be summarised that it was the sheer bad luck of Pitaji that both of his sisters could not get married in good families.

Later, my mother gave birth to her first child, a baby girl who was christened Gita, followed by a son called Anil, and lastly me. I was not only the youngest but also the worst-behaved.

In the meantime, a new development took place that was in the interest of the entire family. I was told that one day my Bade Fufa came to our house and had a discussion with my Bua, his wife, in isolation. Though my Pitaji was against this discussion, he did not intervene. Later, my Badi Bua said to Pitaji that she wanted to go with my Fufa. My Pitaji said that he had taken care of her and her son for the last many years and he could do it forever but if she desired, he would not stop her. Thereafter, Fufa left our home with Bua and Gopal Dada.

As Bua had been in our home for years together, it was an emotional moment as well, but it was not only good for Bua and

Gopal Dada but our family as well. Amma was particularly happy as now she could dream of a happy married life ahead.

It was in 1966, my Pitaji got his transfer order for Bareilly on promotion to Class 2 officer as the Assistant Examiner (currently rechristened as Assistant Director). Our Dhunni Mama or Bade Mama too accompanied us to Bareilly. Amma, for now the first time, could feel the fresh air of independence since her marriage. She was now without the baggage of Buas. So, it was Amma who was the happiest with Pitaji's transfer and she could explore what real happy married life was all about. After reaching Bareilly, we, as young kids, could see a different and happy Amma which we have not seen so far. Her behaviour towards everyone was now more caring and loving including Badi Amma. Our Bareilly residence was very big. Pitaji's office was also in the same building.

Pitaji wanted me and Anil to study in English medium, but the school was ready to take me in Class 2nd but not ready to take Anil in 4th standard.

The school concluded that a kid in class 2nd was more likely to emerge from his Hindi medium background and take up English faster than a student in class 4th. Pitaji refused, and both of us were admitted to Children's Academy, a private school. It was a Hindi Medium school with an emphasis on English. By the fifth grade, I was able to translate stories from Hindi to English.

After reaching Bareilly, Pitaji bought the first Radio of our house, a Murphy Minx Diode valve radio. I vividly recollect Anil and I sitting opposite the radio and listening to songs on All India Radio. The Vividh Bharti had not been launched till then. How innocent the days were that a mere diode valve radio happened to be a prized possession!

Here it would be interesting to narrate a story, it goes as follows.

I was very weak in English while I was in class 2nd and almost every other day Anil would be called to come to my Class and advised in strong words to let Pitaji know of my poor show. One day in English Class, I just made all attempts to hide behind the student sitting just in front of me so that teacher might not see me, oblivious of the fact the teacher was a veteran having a scanner in his eyes and expertise to dig out a hidden student from his so-called bunker. The teacher came close to me and shouted "Come out of the Bunker, Guy and stand up on the bench."

He then called Anil to the Class and while narrating the whole story to him, the teacher told him, "Tell your father what your brother is doing and if things continue like that he would be rusticated from the school."

Anil, already fed up with his regular summoning to my class, saw me standing on the bench and felt humiliated. That day he exploded like anything before Pitaji and reported the entire story. What followed this was unexpected. Pitaji got extremely angry and took off all my clothes and asked me "Get out of the house without any clothes immediately."

I never ever thought Pitaji could react that way. I started crying but Pitaji remained unmoved.

I kept crying and pleaded "Pitaji, please forgive me, I assure you to work hard on my weaknesses."

An unrelenting Pitaji did not accede to my request and shouted, "Just get out."

But then Amma, surrounded by her motherly love, intervened, and got me free from Pitaji's clutches. I assured Pitaji that henceforth, he would not receive any complaints. Since then, I worked on my shortcomings and soon thereafter complaints stopped coming.

Furthermore, I was weak in arithmetic as well. While it did not result in complaints from school as it did in English, it did cause Pitaji to beat me virtually every other day. Not only would he slap me, but he might also hit me with the handle of a hand fan or whatever he might find nearby. Pitaji would beat me during the day, and Amma would be assigned the responsibility of showering me with affection in the evening. "How funny it was for her to caress me in the evening after I had received a beating from Pitaji during the day," Amma would often tell Pitaji.

Pitaji had jokingly coined a special word for the object he would beat me with, and that word was "समझावन लाल (Samjhawan Lal)." He would often say "Should I bring समझावन लाल?"

All these slaps and beatings notwithstanding, I was very naughty and funny. And this led Pitaji to nickname me "चाचा छक्कनलाल खुराफाती" (his self-coined word for a naughty boy). I remember that in my school, prizes would be given to the top three students of each class and they would be garlanded as well. As I always got a rank among the top three, I would get garlanded. I would then reach home with a garland on which not only always made my parents smile with pride in their eyes but they also enjoyed my style of returning from school. I was a good singer as well and always took part in singing competitions at school. I had a fetish for relishing food served in marriage parties and therefore I would join any such party happening around our residence in Bareilly with the chowkidar of Pitaji's office cum residence without informing anyone in the house. Luckily that naughtiness persists in me. I feel a small kid lives in me and that keeps me going even at the age of 62. I consciously believe that I am alive till that kid is alive within me and the day the kid would leave me, I doubt if I would continue doing roles on the stage of drama called life.

But the fact is that Pitaji had inculcated in us the art of working hard, particularly on our weaker points. He always motivated us with stories and simple discussions. He could tell us what the meaning of struggle in life was as he too had come up through that struggle. As a normal middle-class father, he never got satisfied with our performance and made us learn not to get complacent at any stage of life. He embossed in us that we were a learner every day and we could learn from anyone. We were good in studies and always stood among the top three, but when we stood 3rd, he would say why not 2nd, if 2nd, why not 1st, and if 1st, he would say that the marks could have been more.

His thirst for marks and better performance never got quenched and this has made him equally hungry for better results. I remained first class throughout, Anil topped Kanpur university in 1977 while passing out his graduation. Gita too was a very good student. The seeds which our Pitaji sowed in all of us bore fruits when we grew up. All of us got our jobs very easily.

I remember that in Bareilly, Pitaji, being office head was provided with the residence which was attached to his office and just the door of our Main Hall and Pitaji's office chamber separated the two.

One night, Anil sat opposite the Typewriter and Pitaji could see it. He immediately scolded him to get up, yelling "Do you want to be a clerk in life? I will be at my worst if I see anyone sitting before the typewriter any further".

He, for reasons best known to him, had a strong disliking for his kids to become clerks.

How ironic that despite Pitaji's desire that none of his children begins his / her career as clerks, all of us did, Gita with the Post & Telegraph department as a Telephone operator, Anil with Punjab National Bank (PNB) and I with the Reserve Bank of India (RBI) as clerks. I believe destiny had its own intentions. Man proposes and God disposes, as the saying goes.

Pitaji's life journey gave us a lesson that life never comes to us on a platter. It can surprise us both ways. It can lift us and it can bring us down as well. In times of crisis, we need to know that we are braver than we believe we are, stronger than we seem we are, and smarter than we think we are. And on top of it, our Dreams can come true only if we believe in ourselves and do not give up as the beginning is always the hardest.

The struggles of my mother could be categorized in two categories, one, while Pitaji was alive, and second when Pitaji was no more.

Her first struggle taught us that for keeping the family well-knit, personal ambitions and desires need to be put on the back burner. We exist till our family exists, even if it calls for sacrifices of the highest order.

Her second struggle taught us that circumstances are like carpets that need to be kept below our feet and not above. She could make us understand that tough times never last but tough people do and however dark it is, we can always switch on the lights, only if we have patience, endurance, and guts to stand against adversities, so what if it calls for standing alone.

PITAJI UNDER SURGEON'S KNIFE

Things were moving smoothly, and all of us were feeling better in Bareilly. Amma barely had two years of happy married life when Pitaji developed some cardiac problems and had to undergo heart surgery. He went to the All-India Institute of Medical Sciences (AIIMS), New Delhi, with Amma, Mama, and Mami. We kids and Badi Amma stayed back at Bareilly, as our dearest Taiya Maasi had come over to take care of all of us. Those were horrible days full of panic. I was old enough to understand that something serious was going on with Pitaji. Surgery was performed successfully on October 14 1968. After Pitaji's Surgery, we all went to Delhi to see him, who turned too emotional and his eyes welled up. He appeared to be wanting to hug us as he not only loved us beyond measure but had seen us after more than a month also. Because of stitches in his chest and other issues he was denied doing that. He simply put his hands on our heads and kissed us by calling us close to him.

I, being the youngest and the naughtiest, asked him " कैसे हैं आप?" (How are you?) He smiled and indicated he was alright.

We then came back to Bareilly and after a few days, Pitaji too came back with Amma, Mama, and Mami. I was told that Dr Gopinath who performed the Surgery had said to Pitaji after surgery "Misraji you have got another five years of life."

The difficult phase of Pitaji's life as well as ours started thereafter. Pitaji would often have complications but life was moving on and in December 1970 Pitaji was transferred to Lucknow and we rented a house in Buland Bagh. I and Anil got admitted to Government Jubilee Inter College and Gita was admitted to Navyug girls' College.

I remember one incident. In the half-yearly examination, my paper on Algebra was so poorly done by me that in one question it was asked to subtract ABC from 4 ABC, I brought the answer as 4 instead of 3 ABC. Anil in school had seen my paper and advised me of the various blunders made by me. I sensed my mistakes and literally tore the paper. In the evening when Pitaji asked for the paper, I put the onus on Anil saying he took my paper in school and did not return it. Anil denied my allegation, but I took my ground. And when the results were declared I was, as expected, declared failed. It was Amma who somehow managed the fire of Pitaji from falling on me else anything could have happened that day. It was my first and last such poor result.

After the academic year had ended, we relocated from Buland Bagh to A.P.Sen Road, one of Lucknow's most prestigious residential areas at the time. I and Anil got admission to Jai Narain Inter College, and Gita continued in Navyug Girls. In this college, I made some good friends, and one of them was Achal Agnihotri. Despite the separation of almost five decades, we are still very good friends and often meet. One of our neighbours, Mr Dutta, would run a musical orchestra. As I had been an above-average singer, he once asked Pitaji to let me join his orchestra. I did not know why Pitaji did not let me join his troupe. Perhaps that era did not encourage such extracurricular activities. Now I wish if only Pitaji had allowed me to join. I passed 7th and 8th and was studying in class 9th when one night when Pitaji had severe pain in his chest. He got it checked up the next day in Lucknow and everything was found normal. A few days later Pitaji visited Delhi in connection with his official training and got himself checked up in AIIMS. There also nothing unusual was found.

THE PARASOL IS GONE

It was the evening of Wednesday, 24th October 1973, a day before Diwali which we call Choti Diwali. I, Amma, Anil, and Gita were in an open space of residential society along with other co-residents to enjoy the Puppet show being organised by the residents. It being Wednesday, it was the day of the most heard Radio program of that era and which I would seldom miss. It was Binaca Geet Mala, later changed to Cibaca Geet Mala. It used to be aired at 8 PM on Radio Ceylon (now Radio Sri Lanka) and compered by none other than Ameen Sayani, the man with the golden voice and inimitable style. The program comprised of 17 of the most post-popular film songs of the last week.

While we all were enjoying the puppet show, Amma suddenly saw Srivastav ji (Sri S.K. Srivastava, Pitaji's junior as well as colleague whom we called Chachaji) coming all alone. She asked me "Go and see why Chachaji has come and tell him Pitaji is not back home from the office yet."

I reached there and wished him namaste and told him "Chachaji, Pitaji is not home yet."

He said, "Yes, I know but where is your Mausaji 's house?"

"Why are you asking this?" I questioned.

"Your Pitaji is not well and hospitalised." Chachaji replied.

In the meantime, Anil also came over there. He too asked the same question and got the same answer.

I left with Chachaji for Mausaji 's place on the official jeep. We reached Naka Hindola, where Mausaji lived. This place was less than two kms from A.P. Sen Road where we lived. I pressed the doorbell and Mausaji came on the balcony. On seeing me and Chachaji, he asked "Oh, Srivastava ji, you are here, what happened."

Chachaji and Mausaji were familiar to each other through my Pitaji.

Chachaji immediately replied "Misraji (Mausaji's name was Dr A.K. Misra), Misraji is no more."

It was here only I could understand that my Pitaji had expired. I was dumbstruck. Mausaji was shocked too. He came down with Maasi and we drove back home only to see a pathetic scene where Dadi and Gita were crying and Anil, while crying, had broken the glass frames of portraits of Goddess Durga and Lord Shiv. He was shouting about why all this happened to my Pitaji whereas he was a devout Bhakt. Amma was the biggest sufferer of calamity and completely dumb. She was inscrutable and staring blankly.

Maasi saw Amma in this condition and said "This condition of Jijji is not good. She must be made to cry; else it may lead to some psychological problem." Then Maasi held Amma by her shoulder and shook her. Amma came out of subconsciousness and broke down profusely. A wailing Amma brought tears rolling down the eyes of those who were standing nearby. Maasi hugged the wailing Amma but let her vent her emotions. Amma's short honeymoon of a happy married life had abruptly ended. life had come to a grinding halt for her.

While on one hand, I was in shock that I had lost my Pitaji and on the other side wondered how Anil could fathom that Pitaji was no more after a brief interaction with Chachaji. I thought if it was my innocence or foolishness or poor intelligence that I could understand Pitaji's demise only when Chachaji openly told Mausaji. Today's child of my age would certainly have made out which I failed at that time that why Chachaji was enquiring about the address of Mausaji

Later, it was brought to our knowledge that my Pitaji, Chachaji, and Pitaji's Orderly were coming home by office jeep and passing through Kaiser Bagh when Pitaji asked his Orderly to bring some medicines from Khalsa Drug Store (this shop still exists at the same place). When the Orderly got unusually delayed in bringing medicines, Pitaji and Chachaji got down from the jeep and started moving towards the shop, and then suddenly Pitaji fell on the ground. Passers-by thought Pitaji had a fit, but Chachaji told them that he was a heart patient and rushed him to the nearest hospital, Balrampur Hospital. The application of electric shocks notwithstanding, Pitaji could not be revived. He was declared dead. A little later, Pitaji's body was brought home by a hearse having a plate "लाश के वास्ते" (for carrying dead bodies).

Pitaji's body was lying on the floor of our living room whereas my Amna, Gita, Dadi, Mausaji, Maasi, Anil, and others kept sitting beside Pitaji all night. I could not keep my sleep at bay, and slept for a few hours as well. How idiotic or innocent I was that despite Pitaji lying dead in one room, I was sleeping in another room. Perhaps I could not assess the gravity of what I had lost.

Another idiotic act on my part was up for display when a next-door photographer having his Photo studio in Hussain Ganj in the name of Rubi Studio came and clicked photos of Pitaji with us. While everyone was wailing, my eyes had no tears to shed. I had to pretend to look like crying. I still fail to comprehend if I was a little moron then.

The next morning, i.e., 25th of October and Diwali Day as well, after receipt of information through one of our neighbours, Mr. Kulshreshta over telephone, all relatives from Kanpur, i.e., Nana, Mama Mami, Badi Maasi, Bade Mausaji, Mama's in-laws, and others had come up. Pitaji's cousin who had helped Pitaji grow up had also come. Pitaji's body was brought to Bhainsakund (now called Baikunthdham) for cremation. As Yagyopavit Sanskaar of Anil and I had not been done yet, Pitaji's cousin did the all-funeral rites. Anil and I simply kept ourselves on the side-lines. This time tears were rolling down from my eyes as well, perhaps now I could have understood what had happened.

Thus, the chapter of my Pitaji has ended here. My Badi Amma had lost her only son, Amma turned a widow, and we kids became fatherless. Our Parasol had gone forever at 45, certainly not an age to leave the world.

Our Pitaji was a multi-talented man who planted Sanskar seeds so deep in our thoughts and psyches that we still are reaping the harvest. His life is a classic example of rising like a phoenix. A man who lost his father at the age of nine and had the responsibilities of his widow mother, and two unmarried younger sisters never gave up and continued in his life with aplomb. He not only married his sisters but reached a level of Class I officer in state government where he was going to be the Head of the entire UP but as luck would have it, he expired before joining.

Pitaji now lives in our memory only showering his blessings on us always.

But before I close this chapter, I would say that only now I could understand the meaning of Dr Gopinath's words when he said to Pitaji post-Surgery that he had added another 5 years to his life. Surgery was done on 14th October 1968 and Pitaji expired on 24th October 1973. Exactly after 5 years and10 days.

How amazingly spot on Dr Gopinath was!

MOOLI APNE PATTON SE HI BHARI HOTI HAI

A couple of days after Pitaji passing away, our Mama along with his father-in-law, whom everyone including us, called Bade papa came to our house with lots of ration which was enough for at least one year. My mother objected but Mama played the emotional card and said "Jijji, it is my moral duty as I am your brother, so what if I am younger than you? I must ensure that neither you nor my niece or nephews feel wanting in any things." He continued "I cannot bring Jijaji back but what I need to do, I will do."

Amma was speechless and surrendered before him with her welled eyes. Mama also started paying Rs.20 each as pocket money every month to Gita, Anil, and me. At that time even our Pitaji was not paying that much to us. It bears mentioning that but for the timely financial, emotional and moral support of my Mama and Mami at that crucial time, I would have been the worst sufferer as I was just eight standard pass. Mama and Mami acted like Gods for us. I always treated them as our second father and mother respectively.

To cut the working cost of the family, Amma decided to stop the English newspaper "National Herald", which had been a regular morning item in our house. However, our Mausaji objected to the stopping of newspaper and asked Amma "Bhabhi, do not stop the newspapers. It is necessary for kids' knowledge of current affairs, English, and their overall development."

In the meantime, our next-door neighbour Mr. Kulshreshta intervened and said "Bhabhi you may stop expenses on the newspapers. Kids can read the newspaper which comes into our house. After my family has read it, kids can go through it." This way we could read the newspaper, though second hand, and save our expenses on that.

It was brought to our knowledge that before extending help to our family our Mama did have a talk with our Bade Fufa, a literary and political person "You know, jija is no more and his family is now in financial trouble. I plan to extend financial and material support to Jija's kith and kin. I would like you also to come forward and extend some financial help"

Pat came the reply from Fufa "मूली अपने पत्तों से ही भारी होती है" (Radish itself is burdened by its leaves). Thus, my Fufa tangentially declined any help to our family.

As the monthly rent of Rs 110 for the flat was unaffordable for us now, Mama in consultation with Amma decided to bring my youngest, Bitti Maasi to our house so that rent might be shared. As Maasi was also in search of some house on rent, she immediately agreed to it and came to our house with her all-household goods, Mausaji, and two kids, Alok and Ajay. Maasiji was given two rooms and we got confined to one room and kitchen. Toilet/washroom was common.

After coming over to our house, Mausaji started doing weird activities which had put us in difficulties. Maasi also started behaving in a bit of an otherwise manner and never forbade Mausaji from conducting that way. She generally avoided sharing some special dishes with us made by her for her kids. As we were financially not on sound footing, we simply would satisfy ourselves by looking at our cousins relishing the dishes. The relationship with Bitti Maasi had started souring since then and is not sweet even as on date.

Later Mama thought of shifting us to Kanpur. He told Amma "Jijji here in Lucknow, in absence of Jijaji, there is no one to look after the growing kids and finding carefree atmosphere they get spoiled. So, I think it is better to shift to Kanpur after kids pass out from their classes." Amma agreed to Mama's suggestion as she had no other option. In May 1974, results were out and I was 9th pass, Anil 11th and Gita B. A Part I. However, now I feel, had we stayed back in Lucknow, we would have been in a better stage under the guidance of Mausaji (Misraji) as he was a professor of economics in a degree college in Lucknow. It bears mention that two sons of Mausaji, Sanjiv and Soni, are engineers and based in Canada and USA respectively and the middle one, Sharad, a Civil Engineer based in Lucknow. Now thinking about what would have been better is an exercise in futility.

Back to Cradle

It was some day of May 1974, our goods were packed and loaded in a truck. We also boarded the truck to cut costs and reached Kanpur at about 1 AM. We passed through Heer Palace cinema Hall at Mall Road, where Rajesh Khanna starrer film "हम शकल" was being screened.

Amma, Badi Amma, Gita, Anil, and I reached the flat of Post & Telegraph Colony which was allotted to Amma's first cousin, Om Prakash Tewari, our distant mama, and where we were supposed to stay. The rent to be paid was Rs. 60 a month. It was a good but small one BHK flat with Kitchen, toilet, veranda, and roof. It was on the 1st floor in the cantonment area near Murray company crossing. We reached and the entire goods were unloaded from the truck and uploaded to the flat. As it was already a wee hour of the morning, we simply slept on 'as is where is' basis.

The following morning, things began to settle in their respective placements. We did not have double beds, sofa sets, fridges, or almirahs at the time. Apart from cooking gas, we only had two three-hand woven charpoys, one Takht, and some trunks. There was no air conditioning or cooling. The television era had not yet arrived in Uttar Pradesh. Our Badi Maasi resided less than two kilometres away. Bhaiya and Tullu, our cousins, began visiting us on a regular basis and frequently stayed with us overnight. Since very early childhood, Anil and I had a fantastic camaraderie with Bhiya and Tullu as we used to come from Bareilly and Lucknow during summer vacations and enjoy living together at our Nanihaal (Nana's place) in Dhankutti, Kanpur.

Mama used his resources to get us admitted to one of the best schools in Kanpur, Christ Church Inter college. I got admitted to 10th and Anil 12th as we had passed our 9th and 11th respectively from Lucknow. Gita remained attached to Navyug Girls, Lucknow, and would go there only for taking her examinations.

Life started settling here but, of course, with penury, we compromised with life on many counts, be it clothes or quality of food. However, the hard-up days made us learn the value of virtues as well as money.

Om Prakash's mama would often come and stay with us carrying himself weirdly which was a cause of inconvenience for us. But we were helpless and not in a position to take a tough stand against him as it was his flat. On the other hand, it was also true that we were staying there with his consent and paying rent as well. I now feel that he might have permitted us to stay in his flat under the pressure of our Mama and by doing such gestures he was tangentially taking us under pressure to vacate his flat. Till today I could not fathom the reason for his strange contrivances.

During Christ church inter-college school days, one of my Classmates, Hemant Dubey, the rich son of a doctor, started giving feelers to befriend me. One day he took me to FUTU, a Chinese restaurant opposite the Reserve Bank of India. He ordered Veg Fried Rice. Honestly speaking I had never tasted any Chinese dish so far, so found the taste so unique and delicious. The bill for Rs. 4.50 was paid by Hemant and 50 paise was paid as Tip to the waiter. Hereafter, I and Hemant became the fastest friends and we continued classmates till we passed out as graduates. I joined M.Sc. for Chemistry and Hemant opted for Zoology thereafter. I would visit Hemant's house almost daily in the evening and I was like a member of his family. Her three sisters would call me Bhaiya and I would call his mother, Mummy and Papa, Uncle. Hemant had a dog called Romy. He was very much attached to me and whenever I would visit Hemant, I would be greeted by him first.

I once went to Hemant's residence, but he was not there. Poonam, his youngest sister, urged me to wait in Hemant's room because he was expected to return soon. I began to wait for him on the balcony adjacent to the room. Meanwhile, Poonam returned with Tea and Biscuits and placed these on the room's centre table. "Arun Bhaiya, please take tea and biscuits. Bhaiya will be here soon," she added.

I took the tea cup and went to the balcony to enjoy it. I left the biscuits on the table.

I was sipping tea and could not notice when Romy entered the room and there was a sudden sound of the plate falling.

I rushed into the room only to find the plate carrying biscuits on the floor and Romy eating the last of the four biscuits. I bent to pick up the plate and keep it on the table but then suddenly thought that this would make Hemant think that I had gulped all the biscuits. Hence, it was better to leave the plate on the floor as the plate lying on the floor would suggest Romy had consumed the biscuits. So, I left the plate where it was.

And, when Hemant came back, I immediately told him "Your Romy is certainly a naughty dog. He consumed all the biscuits brought by Poonam and dropped the plate on the floor."

Hemant, being a witty person, said "यार खा लिया कोई बात नही, कुत्ते को क्यों बदनाम करते हो" (Friend, it is ok if you have eaten biscuits but why to put an onus on the doggy.)

And then both of us burst into loud laughter.

Our friendship continues even after his leaving for his heavenly abode on the 22nd of April 2021. He was a friend par excellence and always stood not only by me but anyone who came across him. His daughter Shruti, Son-in-Law Niraj and son Anant are outstandingly brilliant and well-placed. I pray Mummy and his wife remain hale and hearty. May Hemant's soul rest in peace. Amen...

Pitaji's terminal dues had now been received and Mama invested the funds in the market. I would bring monthly interest from the persons whom money was invested with. Life started happening a little better. After coming to Kanpur both I and Anil had to resist falling prey to the temptation of rising Pan Parag, a pan masala, which all my cousins etc. were addicted to. I am sure the teachings of Pitaji saved us from getting addicted to such bad habits.

Here in 1975, I passed my 10th standard in the first division and Anil his 12th in the second division. I still remember Gita kissing me on my forehead after the results were out and blessing me. Everyone was happy for me. But no one expected Anil to get a second division as he had been a truly brilliant student. Pitaji's death and the mid-academic year session shift from Lucknow might have hampered his studies. Anil was also very sad about his result. We were all sad for him and offered him our moral support.

In the meantime, Mama decided to shift from his parental home at Dhankutti to a house on rent at Souter Ganj. He asked us to shift to Dhankutti, as we had to pay no rent there. We moved there in June 1976, following the completion of class 11. This shift saved us Rs. 60 a month. Here we had the company of Nana and

Nani as well as our widow Choti Mami, Rajni and her sweet daughter, Reena.

Dhankutti house had problems relating to a short supply of water. Electric supply was more erratic and irregular. It was an awesomely dirty place to live in. No one knew when overflowing sewers would make the roads look like a swimming pool. I had to lift water from the ground floor to the Mezzanine floors for three big drums. It generally took about one hour or so to complete the task. I would keep my study material beside me during this exercise and while waiting for the bucket to fill, I would go through my books. Once while lifting my cycle, I slipped and one of my legs got into an open manhole. I still remember the stink which persisted for several hours even after several showers and a sprinkling of a huge amount of Talcum powder. Perfumes and deodorant were available in the market but unaffordable for us then.

In the meantime, after completing her graduation, Gita got her job in the Post & Telegraph department as a Telephone operator.

PARDA UTH GAYA

Going ahead, during the year1977, a Radio program named "मोदी के मतवाले राही" sponsored by Modi Tyres would get broadcast on Radio Vividh Bharti once a week on a specific day. The program would be related to some story/drama and after that the listeners were asked to coin the title of the story. One day I and Anil had been listening to it and after the program, I in an impromptu manner spoke to Anil "The title of this episode must be "परदा उठ गया." (The curtain had been raised).

Anil agreed to it, and I immediately wrote it on the already-purchased Post Card and posted it the next morning. Two or three weeks later, the winners of this program were announced, and I got the 2nd prize of Rs.50, which was a reasonable sum in 1977. The Prize money came through money order, the most popular mode of sending money those days and it was through the Post Office. It was followed by a letter thereafter. This win just increased my interest in the program, and I started listening to it without fail every week. A few weeks later, after listening to another episode, I titled it "एक ही रास्ता" based on the film released those days. This title was decided after due application of mind. And lo and behold, I was declared the 1st prize winner and the amount this time was Rs 100, double the earlier one.

I gave Amma Rs. 90 for bringing wool for knitting sweaters for me and her and kept Rs.10 with me. Now, this was the time, I decided to give a treat to Hemant out of my own funds. We went to the FUTU restaurant, ordered two plates of Fried Rice, not one and gave the remaining Rs. 1 as Tip to the waiter. That day, I felt a sense of pride that I could give Hemant a treat on my own. Great.

These two wins made me explore other such programs and I found a program sponsored by the Bank of India titled "सवाल आपके जवाब आपके" (Your questions, your answers).

In this program, the questions were sent by the audience by post to sponsors who would select a few questions that would get broadcast on the Radio and listeners would send replies. Out of the replies received the most appropriate replies would be selected and read out on the Radio, of course after two or three weeks. The selected questions and answers were given prizes of Rs. 25. each. I too got hooked on this program and once my question was selected and that was "पैरों तले कुचला फूल गमले में लगे फूल को देख कर क्या सोचता है" (What does a flower crushed under feet think after looking at the flower on a plant in a flowerpot."

Two weeks later my question was selected, and I got Rs. 25 through a money order along with a letter from the Bank of India wherein they congratulated me and requested me to open one account with that money with their bank or any other bank. The unfortunate part was that I could neither hear the program when my question nor when its answer was broadcast.

CATCH-22 SITUATION

In 1977, I passed out 12th and Anil topped Kanpur university in B.Sc. He rather broke the university's record. What a great performance! It made all of us proud. Anil had proved that his class 12th result was simply a one-off aberration and this B. Sc. result was his true mettle. Such performance had vindicated my assessment that the mid-academic year shifting from Lucknow and the sudden and sad demise of Pitaji had taken a toll on Anil's performance in class 12th.

While he was applying for M.Sc.for studying physics, he appeared for a bank clerical test and got selected after an interview. He was allotted Punjab National Bank (PNB). The father of one of his friends Pravin, who was a police inspector, had always been all praise for Anil because of his academic brilliance.

He asked Anil "Do not spoil your career for this pity job of a bank clerk. You are a brilliant student, so continue with your studies and forget about this job."

He further said 'I understand your family has been facing financial hardships since your father expired but I understand this job will not help change the fortunes of your family."

The uncle did not stop here and continued "If you do not mind, I am willing to give you an amount every month equal to your salary. You prepare for IIT and other competitions. When you find you are capable enough, return my money. What I want is to prevent one wonderful talent from going down the drain."

The offer of the uncle was tempting and put Anil in a catch-22 situation. He wondered "Should I accept my uncle's offer or go and join PNB?"

He was fighting a battle of contrasting ideas and opinions within his heart. On one hand, there were prospects for a wonderful career but, of course, not soon and not sure as well, and on the other hand, he had a job in hand with PNB, which was a source of immediate help to his family. A self-respecting and self-possessing Anil preferred to accord priority to joining PNB for the sake of his family. It was a great sacrifice by Anil. I can vouch that, had he accepted his uncle's offer, he certainly would have had a much better career. However, there is no denying that in PNB too, he retired from the honourable Top Executive grade of Deputy General Manager.

It bears mentioning here that since Pitaji's demise, we had very hard-up days and that made Anil join PNB. I still remember that I used to have only two trousers at that time. And, I and Amma would often satisfy ourselves just by eating fried potatoes and parathas. My favourite egg was an occasional delicacy to be enjoyed once in a blue moon only. Anil's earnings, of course, had changed the family's fortunes a lot.

DIL KYA KAREY......

After passing out the intermediate in 1977 from Christ Church Intermediate College, Christ Church Degree College was the obvious choice for graduation. But many people including Anil had opined that I opted for PPN Degree college which, in their opinion, had a better atmosphere for studies whereas Christ Church College was like a club. However, both were having co-education systems. Anil had done his graduation from PPN College and had been currently applying for his post-graduation in physics from there as well.

However, I got admitted to Christ Church College and found that the fashion here was at its peak. It was in vogue for girls to put on jeans, tops, and other modern outfits and this was, perhaps, the reason the college had earned an otherwise reputation among the conservative section of the society. For me, the college had an excellent atmosphere for studies

The ambience of college was quite fascinating for me as, after the 5th standard, it was my first association with girls. Many of my friends from the 12th grade had also opted for Christ Church College. Our subjects were zoology, botany, and chemistry. I had always been good at my studies, so I kept focusing on them. But being a young boy with a romantic heart, girls always fascinated me, and it was quite natural as well. There were many girls in my class, but one girl's simplicity always caught my eyeballs. Her name was Deepika. I got to know she was convent-educated and fluent in spoken English, whereas mine was nowhere near her. As a typical young boy, I had an imaginary dream girl with long hair, big eyes, and a mesmerizing smile with the shyness of an Indian girl. Deepika fitted in beautifully. Aside from the obvious characteristics listed above, what always captivated me in a girl was her elegance, which was defined not by her outfit but by who she was on the inside and how she carried herself. Deepika personified all these qualities. My heart began to skip a beat when I caught a glimpse of her on her way to college and often recollect the lines of a song from Rajesh Khanna and Waheeda Rahman starrer film "Khamoshi."

"मेरा खयाल है अभी झुकी हुई निगाह में खिली हुई हंसी भी है दबी हुई सी चाह में

मैं जानता हूं मेरा नाम गुनगुना रही है वो यही खयाल है मुझे के साथ आ रही है वो

However, she had been unaware of my one-sided crush on her. Despite my liking for her, I could not muster courage to express my love for her and it was a "दिल क्या करे जब किसी को किसी से प्यार हो जाए" (what to do if heart falls in love with someone) like situation for me.

One of our classmates, Archana (unfortunately no more with us now), was her neighbour too. Archana would sit next to me in practical classes. I was quite friendly to her. One day during our informal talks, I said to her "I like a girl in the class."

"Who is she?" she asked with all the girlish curiosity.

"None, I was joking," something held me back, albeit I wanted to say.

"No, you are hiding her name. Tell me. Believe me, I will not tell anyone in the class." She impatiently insisted.

As I myself was desiring to speak my heart out before Deepika but failed to do so, I grabbed Archana's offer thinking this way my suppressed and latent love for Deepika would reach her, through Archana.

"It is none other than your neighbour, Deepika. She is my Crush." I hesitantly spoke.

Archana heard all this silently and looked astounded with eyes broad open. I, however, asked her not to tell anyone else in this regard. In the heart of my heart, I wanted to say that "do tell" it to Deepika but not to anyone else.

However, I knew Archana, being a girl, would not keep the secret information to herself and certainly let Deepika know about this. And, this really happened. She told everything to Deepika. As expected, one day Deepika sent me a message through Archana to see her in the College Library. I went to the library all alone. She was standing there looking too serious. Her body language developed goosebumps in me. The moment she saw me coming she took her position to fire a volley of questions.

"What the hell is this rubbish?' She opened the first fire.

"What! I could not make out." I played innocent.

"You have discussed with Archana about me?"

"Yes, Archana and I sit close to each other during practical class and talk about many friends." I again expressed my ignorance.

"Oh, do not try to be smart with me. Did you not tell Archana that rubbish about my being your crush?"

"Oh, you are talking about that. Yes, I told her that." I said with some air of unexpectedly gained confidence.

I continued "Deepika, if I love a girl then that girl cannot ask me not to love her. Likewise, if I love you then you do not have any right to prevent me from loving you until and otherwise, I behave cheaply. Moreover, Deepika, loving someone is not a crime."

"Oh, do not deliver a lecture. Just tell me why the hell you said it to Archana.? I know her. She would make it an issue of gossip in the class and college." She showed her annoyance.

"Yes, I agree I faulted here and I am sorry for that. But I could not muster courage to come directly to you and express my love. However, I had taken a promise from her not to make it public and I am sure she would keep her promise, at least for your sake." I defended myself but within myself I was terrified what if Archana could not keep her word and make it public.

"Anyways, you may ask Archana not to make this a topic of discussion among the friends. Afterall she is your close friend. I too will ask her to keep her word and not make this sensitive issue public." I suggested as well as offered my help.

"No, not at all. For God's sake you do not poke your nose any further. You have already done the damage. I will manage on my own and talk to Archana. Let us see how things take shape." She emphatically told me with tears in eyes and fear of the unknown on her face.

"Arun, you have unnecessarily created a problem for me." She further said with a mixed bag of annoyance and fear.

A pall of silence had fallen. Both of us were looking sometimes at each other and sometimes here and there.

However, I broke the ice. "Please be rest assured there would be no instance from my side that would be detrimental to your image."

Out of the blue, I had gathered some more courage and told her taking some uncalled-for risk "Deepika do not take me otherwise, I honestly say from the bottom of my heart that the day I stand on my feet, I would send my elders to meet your parents, of course, if we remained friends."

A startled Deepika looked at me expressing how dared I think of parents' meet in our very first interaction, that too when we had discussed some serious issues a just a few moments before.

It looked like my such candid talk and honest confession had gone down well with her and made her open her heart. She said "I discussed all this with my mom and told her about you. She was of the opinion to remain friends only."

After a few minutes of further discussion, we parted. I had an impression that she was hurt not because I had a crush on her but because I preferred to convey it through Archana. And, such an impression brought me closer to her and thereafter our regular hello and hi started happening.

During my B.Sc. days, I had started giving tuition to the kids, one in the morning earning me Rs. 50 per month and the other one in the evening fetching Rs.100. Thus, a total of Rs. 150 was being earned by me side by side with my studies and at that time Rs. 150 was a good sum. This way not only I could earn my pocket money but also contributed, however a little only, to the income of my house which was from Pitaji's pension, interest income on his terminal dues and Anil's handsome contribution through his salary.

In the meantime, Deepika could gather that I was giving tuition to earn my pocket money and supporting my family a bit financially. She once asked me "Are you giving tuition to kids for money?"

'Yes, is there anything wrong with it?' I counter-questioned.

"No, not at all. I, rather, appreciate that you are trying to support yourself and your family side by side with your studies."

"Tuitions give a lot of enjoyment besides giving some money as well." I found a sort of twinkle of love in her eyes for me like in me for her since we met.

" Just thinking about you brings a smile to my face, a twinkle to my eye, and a skipped beat to my heart"

WOH LAMHA NIKAL GAYA......

In 1978, our Mama decided to sell his parental house where we had been living for the last two years with Nana, Nani, Choti Mami named Rajni and her sweet little daughter and our cousin named Reena. He told Amma to shift to Souter Ganj where he had been living for the last two years. He was planning to shift to Civil lines. The Souter Ganj house was on the ground floor. It was in a good locality with a good neighbourhood. There were no issues with water and electricity and the rent was moderate Rs. 50. Though it had started looking small to Mama because of his growing kids, it was enough for me, Amma and Gita. Anil was in Kasganj. I along with Amma and Gita shifted from Dhankutti to Souter Ganj on 5th October 1978. We started enjoying our stay at the house in wonderful company of neighbours specially Srikant Dubli and his wife Archana, Ravi Handa his wife Neera, Abhay Bhanu and his wife Aarti, Vikas Dubli and His wife Bhagyashree, Vijai Handa and his wife Alka besides others.

Before shifting to Souter Ganj, Gita's marriage had already been settled with one handsome guy named Shri Dharmendra Kumar Pandey, who was an employee of Indian Overseas Bank and posted at Kanpur. The marriage was solemnized on 21st, January 1979. After Gita's departure, we felt very lonely as Gita was the life of the house. A few days later, Anil also went back to Kasganj to join back duty and the house was emptier now as only Amma and I were remaining there. The only consolation was that Gita was married in the city itself and our Jijaji, being a thorough gentleman, would often call on us with Gita and stay with us. I always had a good rapport with him. I continued to visit Gita every Saturday till 2004 when she purchased her own house in

Kalyanpur, a far-flung area and about 12 Kms away from my house.

Here, I would like to share that Gita would give me Rs. 60 a month from her salary for my expenses despite my giving tuition. She continued giving me the same till I joined RBI in 1981.

Gita now has two daughters, the elder daughter, Sheebu and the younger one Shilpi. Both are now married, Sheebu has two sons and Shilpi has one.

Over the period, I passed out graduation in 1979 and entered Post Graduation in Chemistry where there were only 13 students, 9 girls, and 4 Boys. Deepika was one of the girls. This period brought me closure to her. Though she had not opened her heart before me yet, her body language and blush on her face while seeing me spoke loudly that her heart had started beating for me. During our free time, all the students would sing songs. As I was a die-hard fan of Rajesh Khanna and Kishore Kumar, I would sing their songs mostly. My friends would say my voice took after Kishore Da a lot. She would also sing wonderfully, and I still remember her singing a song "आजा सनम मधुर चांदनी में हम" from an old classic film. I could see that while singing she was occasionally glancing over me coyly.

Once, during our post-graduation days, we were sitting in the laboratory with no one around. She, out of the blue, asked me "Arun, do you still carry the same sentiments for me that you had in B.Sc.?"

I was taken aback by this impromptu and unexpected question. I got frightened and thought why she had asked this suddenly. I had fallen into a dilemma and did not know whether to say yes, which was the reality, or say no which was out and out a lie.

In sheer panic, I deliberately played innocent as if I could not understand "Which feelings?"

"Those you once conveyed through Archana." She asked.

"Oh, those feelings, no! Not at all. Those feelings have died down."

She appeared unprepared to hear such a reply from me and looked to read into my eyes if I was making a correct statement or lying. Her response made me feel she wanted me to say "Yes."

"Ok," she said and then a few minutes after we parted and. And, immediately thereafter, I started repenting "Why could not I say, yes, I love you?"

I thought I had missed out an opportunity to express my love for her and this time at her behest. I was just repenting and repenting, and suddenly impromptu certain lines just came out straight from my heart.

अब उफ करें या हाय...वो लम्हा निकल गया
उस उठती हुई लहर को...एक खौफ खा गया

However, subsequently, I found her liking for me had reached the next level and occasionally we started visiting each other's houses. Our relationship had become the cynosure of the class by now.

In our farewell party, keeping in view our more than friendly relations, both of us were asked to sing a duet song of a Rajesh Khanna starrer film Aaap Ki Kasam. The song was करवटे बदलते रहे सारी रात हम आप की कसम....

During a friend's marriage function, while sitting side by side and finding a suitable romantic ambience, I asked her "Deepika, it has been long since we have been very close to each other, but you have never said anything openly about our relationship. Tell me now if you love me or have a crush on me."

Deepika looked at me and for the first time she said "Arun I have been having a crush on you since I had a discussion with you in college library but I knew my parents would not give a green signal to our relationship, I have kept my emotions close to my chest."

Though she had confined herself to the word 'Crush' instead of 'Love', it made my heart miss a beat. I remember after that marriage function; I had kept walking around with my friend Sangam Singh for several hours till very late in the night. I even could not sleep that night properly.

EVENTS GALORE

One day while studying for an M.Sc. in 1981, one of my classmates Kavita Rohtagi asked me" Arun vacancies for clerical cadre are out in Reserve Bank India (RBI). I think you would like to apply."

She got the information from her uncle who was in RBI and she knew I was financially hard up.

"Sure, I will apply for the post, please get me a form to apply" I replied.

The next day, she brought the form for applying for the post. I applied, passed the written examination, and made it through the interview as well. It was later made known to us that about 17000 applications were received by RBI and after scrutiny based on applicants' academics, they called about 2000 for Written Test and about 800 qualified for the interview. Out of these 800, about 200 were finally given appointment offers. I stood ranked 30th in the merit list out of 800 who appeared for the interview.

In 1980 Anil had been selected as Probationary Officer (PO) in Hindustan Commercial Bank (HCB). He resigned from PNB and joined HCB at Kolkata. HCB was a private bank having headquarters in Kanpur and allowed candidates above eighteen to apply for the post of POs whereas, in the Nationalised Banks, the minimum age was twenty-one years. After a few months, he was transferred to Kanpur with the efforts of one Shri Shyam Narain Shukla who was an influential Officer in HCB. Anil was posted at the Head office.

In the meantime, our Badi Amma expired at Barabanki, while living with our Badi Bua. I along with Amma went there for her funeral rites. We lost the eldest guardian of our family.

It is pertinent to mention here that just before joining RBI, I got an appointment letter from ACC cements Ltd. as well for the post of Clerk. I remember during the interview one of the board members on coming to know that I had been into giving tuitions, asked me to quit these tuitions. He said, "Mr. Misra, my company does not want its employee to remain preoccupied with some tasks in the morning and evening that do not let him find time for himself to get fresh for the office the next day."

I now compare his statement vis a vis late sitting in banks where top management expects its workforce to sit late and come fresh next morning. A classic example of two contrarian thinking and approaches.

I joined RBI on 9th November 1981 in Kanpur. Here the environment was unlike an office. Overall scenario was carefree and more enjoyable than college. In college we had to study, face the wrath of lecturers, pay fees and on top of it take examinations whereas in RBI, we simply need to come, count, and recount currency notes as per quota, get the note bundles stitched and punched and at the end of the month get money in the shape of Salary. I never had expected such a carefree atmosphere. This task had to be done in two shifts, pre-lunch, and post-lunch but most of us would take the supervisor under pressure to release notes of both shifts in one go so that we might finish the task and go to nearby Nana Rao Park to play cricket with kids playing there. We would take their bat and ball and play, asking kids to field for us. And, if not cricket, we would go back home. Overall, even after playing cricket, we would be home by 2.30 PM.

Anil, who would come home at six in the evening from the office, was aware of my early coming from RBI, thought I was bunking the office as students do in colleges.

I remember once while having some sore relations with Anil, he told Amma "Ask him (Me) to ensure office timings properly or he may lose the job."

"Ask him what I should do when the task is finished, everyone is gone and even the hall where we work gets locked," I told Amma to let Anil know the factual situation.

Thus, I had ample time to study, but I do not know why I preferred to prepare for the test for Probationary Officers in banks to P.C.S. / I.A.S. examinations. I think had I attempted these two examinations; I might have made the grade.

However, In RBI I made some wonderful friends like Vinay, Pankaj, Arvind, Srinath, Rajesh, Dinesh, Vivek, Gautam, Girish, Pramod, Sarfaraaz and others. Many of them are still in regular touch with me.

It would be interesting to mention here that in RBI our post was CNE, which stood for Coin Note Examiner. A few of my high-flying colleagues would often present themselves as Coin Note Engineers thereby idiotically concealing their true identities of being clerks and making fake impressions on others.

After Anil's transfer to Kanpur, Shyam Narain Shukla who was instrumental in Anil's transfer back to Kanpur from Kolkata started making efforts to get his eldest daughter Abha married with Anil. As Anil earlier used to give tuition to Abha and her sisters when we lived in Dhankutti, he was against this relationship and said it would give some wrong message about him that as a teacher he had affairs with his student and ultimately got married as well.

All efforts to get him to change his mood fell apart. However, I do not know whose advice ultimately prevailed upon Anil and got him ready to tie the knot with Abha.

After pre-marriage functions, the date of marriage was fixed on 9th December 1982. It was a moment of joy for the entire family. All preparations were in full swing and the marriage function was performed at the newly built house of one of Shyam Narain Shukla's friends, opposite Green Park Stadium, Kanpur. Anil's married life started going on smooth sailing. Everyone was happy in the house. Amma had got a bahu and I had a beautiful and caring Bhabhi. The only sad point in Anil's and Bhabhi's life had been that they could not become parents and I could not hear the sweet word "Chacha." I had always been fascinated by kids calling Chacha to their Chachas.

It is interesting to mention here that Anil, during the days of his giving tuitions to Abha once had gone to Mumbai to appear for an interview for the defence forces. I was deputed by Anil to take classes in his absence. It was for about seven days or so. I recollect, during the entire period, there were fewer studies but more laughter all around.

A few months thereafter my mother had started to nudge me to tie the knot. As I was in love with Deepika, I would avoid this and always tell her that Anil had just got married and as he was older than me by almost two years, I must be given that much time-space.

AS IF I HAVE BEEN DUPED

One day perhaps in the first week of June 1983, I got a message from Deepika to see her at Pioneer Pen Stores, Navin Market, the poshest market of Kanpur. On the prefixed day, I reached Pioneer Pen Stores and immediately thereafter she too made it there. We exchanged pleasantries and discussed each other's well-being.

I asked her "Well, any specific reason for today's meeting?'

"No, nothing specific. We have not met for the last two months; so, I wanted to see you and talk to you." She replied.

Immediately thereafter I said, "Ok, but Deepika, our meeting this way serves no purpose until and otherwise there is any likelihood of it reaching its destination. I think you understand what I mean. And, that is why I plan to come to your house and meet your parents regarding our relationship."

"What are you saying...are you crazy Arun?" A dumbfounded Deepika enquired with awe on her face.

"Yes, I mean it. I find it difficult for me to concentrate on my studies as you always play at the back of my mind. I feel I have been wasting myself by doing a clerical job whereas, I am sure, I deserve much more. It is high time both of us took a hard-headed call to seal the fate of our relationship either this way or that way. This middle path is neither in your interest nor mine." I emphatically replied.

"Arun my parents, particularly my dad, are too conservative and into caste. They would never give approval to our relationship as I am a Kayasth and you are a brahmin. And if you come to my place, he would not only say a big No but make it difficult for me also, leave alone our meeting in the future." She said with fear in her eyes.

"Let it be. If they will not agree to my proposal, it is fine. At least I would focus on my studies to make my career. And, if now I do not come to your place, then throughout my life I would repent if only I had visited you, your parents might have given their nod to our relationship. Moreover, I do not believe in the caste system, you know." I put up my point.

She looked bewildered and astounded, not in a position to say yes or no to my proposal. Perhaps she had been cursing herself why she invited me to Navin Market in the first place. Ultimately, notwithstanding her reservations, she came out of the dilemma and willy nilly agreed to my point. Saturday 11th June 1983 at 7 pm was fixed for my visit to her place.

I told two of my closest friends, Hemant Dubey (who unfortunately is no more now) and Sangam Singh, about my plan. They, too, were taken aback by my plan but remained silent. I asked for their company while I visited her house to stave off any unpleasant happenings; if at all this happened. However, I was sure that such probabilities were remote. Both agreed to stand by me solidly. I told Amma about this program, and though she was surprised at my decision, she did not stop me but certainly advised against taking some extreme steps if things did not go my way. Amma had a liking for Deepika, who had also visited my house a couple of times, and had no issues with a Kayasth bahu. On 11th June at 7 PM sharp, I along with both Hemant and Sangam reached her place and rang the bell. Fortunately, it was she who opened the door.

We said "Hi! How are you, Deepika?"

I am fine. What about you all." she replied.

"We all are fine," We collectively replied and entered the living room.

Thereafter, we started sharing lighter moments. Out of the blue, Hemant and Sangam started looking a bit panicky and asked me "Arun, the situation looks normal and cool. We think it is better we leave so that you may have some personal and private talks with Deepika and her parents."

I could sense they were getting a bit jittery.

"Ok, you two may leave but wait for me somewhere outside." I allowed them to go.

Both Hemant and Sangam left her place with the sign of relief on their faces. Now it was only me and her in the room

"Deepika, Should I go ahead with my plan or drop it?" I tested her.

"No, you move ahead as per your plan. Let us see what destiny has in store for us." She appeared to be bolder now.

A few minutes after, Aunty, I mean her mom, had come into the scene. Deepika introduced me to her "Mummy he is Arun. She is my mom, Arun."

"I can understand she is Aunty." I replied in a lighter vein.

I wished Aunty and started making ground for the purpose I had come.

I said, "Aunty you did not come to my brother's marriage."

She replied, "I was not well beta, but Deepika did make it to the marriage."

"Yes, Aunty, but I was expecting you all there," I responded.

In the meantime, a phone call came, and Deepika went with the phone to another room. Those days there were no mobile phones. Her landline phone had a long cable attached so that it could be moved from one room to another.

Now only me and Aunty were in the room.

Without wasting any further time and before my courage gave in, I straightforwardly and bluntly told her with my heart in my mouth "Aunty, I want to marry Deepika."

I thought Aunty would stand up in rage and say "What! Have you gone crazy…is this the way of coming with a proposal…where are you parents and elders...just get lost."

Contrary to my assumption, Aunty remained calm and composed. She expressed no signs of exclamation, rather replied very normally, "Beta, you know, Deepika's papa is too much into the caste and would never give his green signal to this relationship."

Such a cool reply from Aunty was unexpected. I was shocked how Aunty had played so coolly. After all, a boy in his early twenties had come to her place with a proposal of marrying her only daughter that too all alone. It was quite like a scene from a romantic Bollywood movie where the hero often does such antics.

"What's there in a caste Aunty?" I countered as Aunty's incredibly cool reply helped me gain some confidence and courage.

"I understand beta, but you do not know her father." Aunty coolly made her point again.

"You know Aunty, castes were not created by God. He has simply brought us to the world as human beings and made the only distinction as boy or girl. This caste system is the brain-child of us only, I mean humans." I forcefully put forth my argument as a philosopher.

"I agree beta. But Deepika's father is a different person and never thinks of marriages outside his caste." Aunty remained unperturbed.

"Then why do you not make him understand the ground reality?" I asked

"Beta, I do not, or for that matter, no one in my family has that much courage to talk to your uncle in this regard," Aunty replied still without losing her temper.

"Aunty, consider one situation. Supposing when I was born, my parents would have died, and I was brought up by a Muslim family, then had I been Muslim or a Hindu? I think everyone would have called me by a Muslim name. No one could have recognised that I was a Hindu boy. So, it puts weight in my arguments that there is nothing like religion or caste. It is simply our creation and a cause of tension and division in society." I had played my most potent card, philosophically again.

Aunty appeared not to buy any of my arguments and stood her ground "All is fine beta, but you do not know Deepika's father. He is very rigid in his conviction. Taking up the matter with him means vitiating the air of the house plus it may be detrimental to Deepu's interest. He is genuinely a tough guy."

"Aunty...." I expressed my anguish.

"Sorry beta," Aunty replied as if she had sympathy for me.

I thought there was no logic in putting any further argument, therefore, I said "It is alright Aunty." I got up, said namaste, took her leave, and left Deepika's house without waiting for or meeting her.

I was out of her house now thinking my love life was over now forever and started moving towards my home. Immediately, both of my friends appeared again, and I told them the outcome and they expressed their sympathy.

I was moving back home with a heavy heart thinking I had been duped by Deepika. To me, it looked like a well-planned strategy and scripted drama on the part of Deepika. I thought that after my plan to visit her house, she might have planned and taken her mom in confidence to let me come in the house and speak my heart out. She might also have requested her mom to listen to my words very quietly without losing her cool, and finally, deny my proposal putting the onus on her Daddy's rigidity with the caste system. This way, I thought, Deepika had made sure to kill two birds with one bullet. First, not only would I go back with the impression that Deepika was in love with me and wanted our relationship to go to the next level but her Daddy came as a roadblock and sabotaged all things, secondly, I would not feel insulted, and our relationship would continue. It is relevant to mention here that the timing of that telephone call too had added weight to my doubts. I was heading home step by step with a heavy heart feeling duped by Deepika.

Bade Mauj Ki Naukri Hai

In 1984 I appeared for a written test for SBI Associate Banks' POs which I qualified and was called for an interview at Lucknow in early 1985. The interview board had 5 members, and I can swear that it was my best interview ever. It lasted for no less than 40 to 45 minutes and my confidence was on a high pedestal.

During the interview, one of the board members asked me "Well Mr. Misra, you are in RBI. Tell me frankly at what time you get free from the office."

This was an unusual question which was unexpected from the board member. My sixth sense suddenly got awakened and guessed this member might be from RBI, aware of the facts, and lying to him would cost me dear.

"I generally get free very early and by 2 PM or so I am home," I replied honestly.

I still remember the scene when, after listening to my reply, another member of the board leaned on the shoulder of the questioning member and whispered, which was faintly audible to me as well, "बड़े मौज की नौकरी है." (This is an amazing job.)

Suddenly one more but expected question popped up "Well, then you have ample time with you, what do you do in that time?"

Perhaps the Almighty God was with me on that day, and I replied "Sir, I study, and the result is that I am sitting before you."

This reply from my side played the trump card and I realized that it had gone straight into their hearts and they had framed positive opinions about me. As the interview progressed, the board discussed political and apolitical issues, they asked "What're your hobbies, Mr. Misra?"

"Besides Singing, playing cricket and Table Tennis, I love writing short stories," I replied.

Pat came the next question "who is your favourite Short Story writer?"

As I was not a voracious reader and not aware of any specific short story writer, I instantly said "I do not follow any author. What I feel or observe, I write." The question-answer session somehow boosted my morale to such a level as I mustered courage and requested the interview board "May I ask one question, sir?"

"Yes, why not?" they consented.

"Ours is a secular country, so why are we supposed to fill in our religion in all the applications?" I asked.

Board members looked amongst themselves and one of them replied "It is because of keeping demographic data."

"Is it necessary sir? Why keep such data which does nothing but, of course, divides the society for sure."

The members of the board appeared clueless and looked amongst themselves.

Without offering any answer to my question, they said "Well Mr. Misra. All the best.

It was a clear indication that the interview was over. I came out of the interview room after saying thanks to them and wishing them as well. I was satisfied with my performance in the interview and quite sure of making it through.

Getting Ready to Mingle

On 11th June 1983 when my proposal of marrying Deepika was turned down by her mom, my opposition to marriage had started dying down. But I always avoided any talks in this regard as I had framed an opinion that if no Deepika, then no marriage, and I could succeed in deferring it till early 1985 on the grounds that let me be an officer prior to marriage. But the pressure to get married had started coming on me indiscriminately. Two years of hiatus after Anil's marriage had passed off too.

By now, I had appeared for interviews for the posts of POs in SBI associates and Allahabad Bank also. I was optimistic about making it through the interviews, particularly that of SBI associates.

It was in the third quarter of 1985 when one of our neighbours Mr. R.N. Shukla and his wife Meena, who were in distant relation to us through my Mami, discussed with Amma about my marriage with their niece. I addressed both as Chacha and Chachi respectively.

Meena Chachi would often say to Amma "Bhabhi, since your arrival in Souter Ganj, I had been longing to get your younger son (me) married to my niece, who lives in Lucknow."

So, the horoscopes' matching process was undergone, and thereafter a date was fixed on which my family was supposed to see their niece. Her name was Sandhya, nicknamed Reena. Reena's father Shri Shri Narain Shukla was Dy. Director in Fisheries department of UP Government and posted at Faizabad. Besides her father, there was her Mummy and two brothers,

Guddoo and Reeshu. Reena was the eldest among the kids in the family.

On the prefixed date, Reena along with her mother and brothers reached Meena Chachi's place. Which was upstairs my house. I have always maintained that when I could not get married to someone I liked, there was no point in seeing a girl, rather any girl chosen by the family would do.

I, therefore, told Gita "You all see and finalize the girl. I should not be called upstairs to see the girl."

Gita vehemently opposed my suggestion and said "This is being done for your marriage and final yes or no must come from your side. We can only give our opinions."

Amma, Gita, Bhabhi, Mami, and her younger son, Mikkie went upstairs.

After 15 minutes, my cousin Mikkie came down and asked me "Dada, Gita didi has called you to see my would-be Bhabhi."

I had to go up unwillingly. I saw Reena sitting there with well-shampooed and open hair. She was beautiful and looking downwards. There was neither any eye contact nor any question-answer session between us.

I found one thing unusual there. Reena's father was conspicuous by his absence. It made me think that perhaps he too was averse to clerks like my father and as such not interested in getting her daughter married with a clerk. Reena later told me that he was in fact against our relationship initially but once there was a green signal from our family, he somehow relented.

Within a few minutes, I came down followed by my family members a few minutes later.

I was asked by Gita and Mami "What is my opinion about Reena."

Reena was much better than me in all respects. She was beautiful and there was no reason to say No. So, I said "It is my considered opinion that once a girl has been seen, she must not be rejected until and otherwise something really calls for rejection. As Reena has no adverse features that might compel me to say No. so It is Yes from my side."

Bhabhi appeared to have some reservations about Reena based on her wheatish complexion. However, others were in sync with me.

After a short gap, Meena Chachi came down and asked my Mami "Manju (Mami's nickname) what's the opinion about my Reena?"

Mami replied, "it is yes from our side."

Meena Chachi jumped in happiness and said "मंजू तुमने मेरी इज्जत रख ली" (Manju you saved my honour)

Thus, my marriage to Reena was finalized and it was decided to find out dates for further ceremonies.

This way the way for Reena was opened for entering my life

In a Dilemma

In the third quarter of1985, SBI Associates PO's result was out and I got the appointment in State Bank of Bikaner and Jaipur (SBBJ). I was supposed to join Kaushal puri, Kanpur branch. I was incredibly happy, and my RBI colleagues congratulated me. It bears mentioning that the job of Bank PO was a prestigious one at that time and considered no less than IAS. During those days young boys and girls would prefer IAS/PCS/PO, besides Engineering and Medical.

I submitted my notice of resignation to the RBI and came back home. After having Lunch at home, I had an afternoon siesta. When I got up in the evening, I started feeling depressive goosebumps.

I thought "Currently I have been posted in Kanpur, but this is a transferable job that too across the country, I would not remain in Kanpur always and one day might be transferred to some other far-flung areas."

Besides, I thought "How will I live all alone as I am not only homesick but cannot live without Amma also?"

As the youngest member of the family, I was not only adored by Amma, but I also adored her. Furthermore, my love for her knew no bounds, and I never imagined living without her. Furthermore, because Anil and Gita were not around, I received extra attention from her, making me too sensitive to consider my life without her.

"But it is a question of your career. You have always wanted to be an officer. Pitaji too never wanted any of us to be clerks. It is a chance to come out of clerical stigma. After all, you had worked hard to get selected and performed exceedingly well in the interview. So come on, just go get it." My conscience pushed me hard as a war of words was going on within me.

Notwithstanding all this, all efforts to convince myself fell apart. I ran back to RBI and met my young Trade Union leader Jiwan Kumar Chaudhury, whom we called Dada.

"Dada, I want my resignation notice back. I do not want to join SSBJ as I cannot think of living alone away from Kanpur without my mother." I said to Dada.

"But you have to join at Kanpur, why are you talking about going outside Kanpur?" Dada asked.

"Dada today it is Kanpur, tomorrow it will be somewhere else. Please help me get my notice back." I forcefully said.

"OK right now go back, think it over before you take a final call. By the way, you want to let go of an opportunity many a friend of yours are dying for." Dada tried to make me understand. I came back home.

I took two-three days to think about what to do but failed to reverse my opinion of taking my resignation notice back and ultimately withdrew my resignation notice.

After a few days, a clerk of that branch of SBBJ, Govind Mishra, came to RBI in connection with the clearing of cheques. He was aware of postings of some POs in his branch. He was known to Dada and enquired about me from him. He met me and asked, "Why did you not join?" He continued "Four persons were to join, three boys and one girl. Only the girl has joined."

He suggested that I go to his branch and meet the girl who had already reported so that I could revisit my decision of abstaining from joining SBBJ.

At his suggestion, I went to the SBBJ branch and met that girl. She was Neeta Jain.

"Please do join. It is a good place to learn" She got me almost convinced to join SBBJ.

The next day, I again submitted my resignation notice to the RBI. After a few days, the depressive feelings of living without Amma surrounded me again which resulted in the re-withdrawal of my resignation notice again, of course with the help of Dada.

But this time I was chided by the management like anything. I was categorically told, "In the future, if you submit your resignation notice, it must be one month prior to the date of leaving the bank and not withdrawn, otherwise the bank may take appropriate action against you."

I listened to the words of management. As I had nothing to say, but kept mum and came out of the chamber with a sigh of relief.

SOME ADVICE TO BE GIVEN EARS

In 1985, Anil started thinking of having his own house, rather our family's house, and it was a promising idea as well for the entire family. After all, which family does not want to live in its own house!

Pitaji had purchased a two hundred square yards plot in K-block Kidwai Nagar, Kanpur decades back and after Pitaji, Amma had been paying its instalments. Anil had been planning to build a house on this Land. Once Bade Papa, Mami's father, had advised "Anil why not build a house on the parental plot by using my money and run your house either with your or Arun's salary and the other salary be used to service my interest-free loan?"

Anil did not purchase his idea as he wanted to take a loan from his Bank. As my job in RBI was less than 5 years, I was not eligible for a loan whereas Anil was entitled to one from his bank. But as the title of the plot was in the name of Pitaji, the loan was not possible. For a loan, a clear and absolute title in favour of Anil was required. Anil was advised to file a suit in the court against Amma, Gita, and me, the three surviving legal heirs of Pitaji besides Anil, where we all must depose to have agreed to our division of properties as per our mutual family settlement.

As such Anil told me "I will send notices to you, Amma and Gita and in court, you all simply need to depose that as per our mutual family settlement, the Land Property had been given to Anil and the remaining had been shared amongst us three." In fact, there was no other property barring this land bequeathed by Pitaji. The notices came calling after a few days. On the scheduled date we reached the court and all of us deposed before the judge on oath

"We will speak the truth and nothing but the truth. As per our mutual family settlement, the Land Property has been given to Anil and the remaining properties have been shared by us."

A decree was passed by the court and Anil was declared the absolute owner of the Parental Land. I and everyone in the family were happy as our dream of the family home was coming true. And there was nothing to feel adverse about it as well, keeping in view Anil's past track record of honesty.

However, Srinath Dixit, my school-time friend as well as RBI colleague was the only exception who had all along been advising me against this deal. He did say time and again "Arun, it is your family issue and I do not have any locus standi in it, but I do not see any logic in relinquishing your share in the parental property in favour of your brother. This way you are not only jeopardizing your interest but also the future rights of your kids who will take birth in due course of time."

He further said "You respect and trust your brother; it is good but what looks good today may not look good tomorrow. After your marriage and passage of time, you never know what twists and turns happen in life and how things take shape?"

That time I simply disagreed with Srinath Dixit and shrugged off his advice saying "No dear! My brother is different and genuinely an honest person. He will never hurt mine and my future kids' interests." At that time, I found Srinath's apprehensions impermissible and extremely exaggerated, unlikely to happen in real life.

However, as the years went by, I realized that Srinath was spot on and it was a mistake on my part to have been swayed away emotionally at that time. I would occasionally repent my mistake but it was Reena's magnanimity as she would always pacify me "Why do you lose peace of mind? You must be proud of yourself that notwithstanding having been bequeathed nothing by Pitaji, except of course moral values, and starting from the scratch, you could reach a level where you are now. You are an owner of a house purchased by you entirely on your own without anyone's financial help barring your bank loan and have been shouldering your responsibilities single-handedly, taking due care of Amma and our two kids, besides me. I am happy and feel proud that I am the wife of a man who is genuinely self-made."

Now my considered opinion is that we must not be carried away by emotions in such matters and a piece of genuine advice from a friend or anyone must seriously be given ears.

I GOT HITCHED

As our Souter Ganj house was too small to accommodate Amma, Anil, Bhabhi, me, and my future wife, Anil had shifted to an accommodation in Civil lines under Bank lease with Bhabhi.

My marriage had been finalised; the date was fixed for 12th March 1986. It was solemnized at a hotel at Mall Road, Kanpur. Reena's family had come down to Kanpur from Lucknow. Most of her relatives were based in Kanpur. Her family had arranged a few rooms in Hotel Shivoy for the stay of my family and friends. It was a good reception, and everything went Well.

The Jaimal ceremony was about to be done, when suddenly one of my college mates and RBI colleagues as well, Shrinath Dixit, reached the stage in a drunken stage and asked Reena "भाभीजी आप कैसी हैं?" (How are you Bhabhi ji?)

The draught of drunken air reached Reena. She immediately started feeling dizzy and nearly fainted when I held her from falling. Her close ones at the stage took her back to her room in the hotel.

This incident brought an eerie silence in the gathering. As often happens in such cases, people sitting had started making their wild guesses. Some thought it was because of weakness as Reena had been on fast since morning, some speculated too wildly that she was a patient of hysteria. However, after a few minutes, silencing all speculations, Reena was back with us and Jaimal got done with all fanfare. During the night all rituals of marriage were done and after taking seven rounds of pious fire, I and Reena became husband and wife with a promise that we would stand by each other till our last breaths.

The next morning the Vidayee program was done and I along with Reena came to Anil's house at the civil lines. After post-marriage rituals at Civil lines, we reached our house at Souter Ganj. Bhabhi had reached there prior to us and rearranged my Souter Ganj house which was in a mess for many days as we had stayed with Anil for marriage.

On the very first night, after entering the room I saw Reena very closely for the first time. I found her beautiful with sharp features and big eyes. She had all the features I had always imagined in my dream girl. She was quite nervous, and it was quite natural as well. I discussed her hobbies and talked about her.

I asked her "Reena there was no eye contact between us on the day when we first met at your Chacha's house and I observed that you did not try even once to see me, whereas I glanced at you and found you stunning. How could you then give your consent to marry me?

My appreciation of her beauty appeared to have been liked by her and she blushed. She replied "Who asks a girl about her liking? But I had seen your photograph and that was enough for me to say yes. However, I certainly had a glance over your feet which were too fair for me to believe." I had nothing but to laugh hearing that and said "How innocently foolish of you Reena!" And then both of us burst into laughter, though mild.

Besides, talking to Reena, I compared her with Deepika and found her no less than Deepika. I also thought if I should tell Reena about Deepika or not. After a few minutes of a tug-of-war between contrarian opinions, my conscience prevailed upon me. I decided to tell Reena all about Deepika and the fidelity between husband and wife demanded that as well.

I said, "Reena, I want to share something with you but I am in a dilemma. I am afraid of how you would take it, particularly on our first night."

"What?" A nervous Reena questioned with anxious eyes.

"While studying in college I had a crush on a girl and her name was Deepika. And, I even went to her residence with a marriage proposal but her parents declined my proposal." I could gather courage.

Reena was caught unawares and looked bewildered.

"Do not worry, we have not been in touch since I visited her last in 1983 and I even do not know where she is now." I tried to placate Reena and her worries.

Reena looked at me with a plastic smile on her face. But her face was speaking that my disclosure had not gone well with her.

I continued "Reena if I wanted, I could have kept this off from you but as you are my wife, my life partner, I thought I must tell you all this in clarity so that if you, somehow, happen to get any information about her from other sources, you may not feel I had cheated you."

Reena looked reassured after this statement of mine and smiled. I thought my honesty in our relationship had won her heart. However, simultaneously, I was afraid this disclosure might have let some suspicion creep into her heart as well.

The next day, the 14th March, was fixed for our post-marriage reception party, which we called At Home. It was very ironic that it was me who was looking after arrangements for my reception party with my RBI friends, neighbours, and Hemant in the nearby Durga Puja Park. It was even more ironic that Reena was in the kitchen preparing food. Normally, other members of the family like Gita and Bhabhi must have been in the kitchen instead of Reena, at least today.

Anil, Bhabhi, Gita and Jijaji, and others came in the evening. This incident had not only hurt me, but Reena had taken it to heart and later would often say to me "Do you not feel that it was unusual for a new bride to be in the kitchen making lunch on the day of her post-marriage reception party?

This sarcastic query from Reena could never find a suitable reply from me nor could I ask Gita and Bhabhi where they had been at noon on that day.

Once Reena could find my collection of greeting cards exchanged between me and Deepika as well as friendly letters and a small college diary. She very calmly gave it to me saying sarcastically "Take care of your precious items."

The small college diary was given by the college to every student. I would often jot down my feelings or other things on it.

In one of the lines written by me in the diary, Deepika was found to be saying "Arun, the love and affection you have for me is not good as you will find it difficult to give the same love and affection to your wife. So, hold your emotions."

This sentence, though, was written by me more than a decade back and was irrelevant now but it was perhaps taken as relevant by Reena's heart, and she would often dig sarcastically at me.

KAHAN PHANS GAYE

My post-marriage life started moving smoothly and we had been living happily. There was wonderful compatibility between me and Reena. By June 1986 I got an appointment letter from Allahabad Bank, informing me of my appointment in the bank and posting place and date of joining were Orai and 14th July, respectively.

I submitted my resignation notice to the RBI on 9th July 1986. This time I did not take my resignation notice back as I was not alone now. Reena was there to accompany me. I was relieved on the 12th. RBI staff gave me a lovely farewell at Shalakha restaurant on the ground floor of Hotel Meghdoot, the best hotel in Kanpur then. The friends who were present there included Dinesh Srivastava, Vinai Saxena, Rajesh Sekhari, Srinath Dixit, Vivek Srivastava, etc. Dinesh had also appeared for the interview of PO with me but could not make it to the selected candidates. He at that time said "Arun you have got your career made. I, unfortunately, could not make it to successful candidates. Now I must undergo another five years before I get to appear in Officer Grade "A" Written Test in RBI as a Staff candidate." However, Dinesh later took promotion in RBI after eight years in 1994 and retired as the General Manager and Banking Ombudsman, UP. He would now say

"अरूण, तुम दुर्भाग्य से इलाहाबाद बैंक पीओ के लिए पास हो गए थे मैं सौभाग्य से फेल हो गया था नही तो ज्वाइन कर लेता और तुम्हारी तरह जगह जगह ट्रांसफर होता रहता।" (Arun, it was your Bad luck that you got selected as Allahabad Bank PO and my Good Luck that I failed otherwise, I too would have joined and travelled multiple places like you on transfers.)

My golden days with RBI were over and I left Kanpur on the 13th with my wife and my cousin Sharad for Orai by bus in the evening and stayed at Neelam Lodge. I can vouch I had never seen before and thereafter such a nasty place to stay.

On 14th July I reached the branch with my Dossier at about 10 AM. The main entrance of the branch was locked from within. I came to know that the cash was being taken out from the strong room and hence the gate was locked. I was unaware of this practice. In the meantime, a gentleman came from behind. While looking at the Dossier in my hand he enquired "Are you joining today as a new recruit?"

"Yes," I replied.

"Well, I am M.S. Sengar, an employee of this branch" He introduced himself and shook hands with me.

"Which post are you joining for?" He asked again.

"PO." I immediately replied.

He looked at me with reverence as the post of the PO was a prestigious one then.

"Is this your first assignment or have you been working somewhere before this?" He raised another query.

"Yes, I was in RBI, Kanpur," I replied with arrogance.

On hearing my reply Sengar ji shrugged his shoulders and turned his head the other way whispering in disdain "कहां फंस गए?" (Where I have trapped myself.)

This small line from Sengar ji pierced through my heart and my dreams almost got shattered. I questioned myself "Have I made a wrong decision?"

Now, I had no other option but to report to the branch head. The RBI days had now gone into history. As the cash had been taken out, the main channel gate was now open. I entered the branch premises and got another blow. There was a total mess all around. The branch looked completely untidy, and things were littered here and there. I compared it with the ambience and maintenance of RBI and cursed myself for quitting RBI.

I reached the chamber of Branch Head and here the bigger blow was waiting for me to witness. The Branch Head and one officer, later I got to know that he was Branch Head's Deputy, were in a verbal duel in full volume. I mustered courage and gently entered Branch Head's chamber and told him "Sir, I am Arun Misra, I have to join as PO here." The disturbed branch Head asked one of the junior officers to take me to one other room. I went there and remained there till Lunch and came back again within half an hour. I remained in that room doing nothing till 4 PM when I was called by the Branch Head to his chamber.

"You might have felt very unusual witnessing the morning scenes at the branch?" Branch Head asked me.

Though I wanted to say "yes, I was," I diplomatically said, "sir, I am from RBI and hence used to all these happenings."

The Branch Head smiled as if he could smell the sarcasm between the lines of my statement. I took out my papers from the dossier I had brought with me.

"OK, you may go now and come tomorrow and then your learning will start."

"Thank you, sir." I said and left the branch for the dirtiest place of stay but the words of Sengar ji kept resonating in my ears "कहां फंस गए?"

Even today when Sengar ji (who also lives in Kanpur) meets me, his face makes me reminisce his three words "कहां फंस गए"

In the Orai branch, the Branch Head had a penchant to sit late in the evening approximately till 7 pm which was quite traumatic for me as in RBI, I was used to getting free latest by 2 pm. Adjustment to this time schedule was also a challenge initially but as the time passed by, not only it had become a part of my routine but also of my wife's. Over the years, a stage had come that even leaving the office by 7 pm looked like bunking the office. The funny part was that when I would reach home early, though as late as 7.30 pm, my wife would ask "So early, Are you alright?"

In the Orai branch, unfortunately, I failed to learn anything of banking as the Branch Head simply used me as a reliever and all my requests to let me learn fell on his deaf ears.

In the meantime, HCB got merged with PNB and Anil had to leave Kanpur for Delhi to report at the Head Office of PNB. Now it was for Bhabhi only to look after the house construction going on in Kidwai Nagar. After almost seven months' stay at Orai, I was transferred to Rania, a branch 30 km away from my house, in the month of February 1987.

My transfer from Orai to Rania branch meant I could stay at my Kanpur residence and commute daily between Kanpur to Rania and back.

On the very first day of my journey to Rania, I boarded a Roadways bus from Chunni Ganj bus station. As was my habit, I enquired from one or two passengers "How much time do buses generally take from here to reach Rania and what is the frequency of availability of buses?"

A passenger sitting next to me saw me asking this query to a couple of people and asked me "Are you Arun Misra?"

"Yes, I am," I replied. I wondered how this man could know me.

"I am Ravi Kumar, Manager Rania branch of Allahabad bank." Before I could ask, he had given his introduction.

"I live in Parmat and commute between Kanpur and Rania daily." He continued.

Parmat was about a kilometre or so from my place. I was happy to know that as the manager commuted daily, so it would not be a problem for me to commute daily. As per the bank's Service Regulations, every official was required to stay at his place of posting and leave the station only after seeking permission from the Competent Authority.

During our talks, he asked me "Do you know how to write a Long Book, a Day Book or make Weeklies or for that matter about basic banking?"

"No sir, I do not know. I have been completely misused in Orai. I was not allowed to sit on counters to learn how accounts are opened, how cheques are debited or credited in the account" Pat came the reply from me.

I continued "You may treat me as a fresher who is joining in your branch. Well, I have worked in the cash receipt department."

Ravi Kumar ji looked at me with awe and I thought he was shocked that the officer reporting at his branch was blank in banking even after seven months of probation in a Semi-Urban branch.

He replied "Ok no issues, it is alright. You may learn all that you could not learn in the Orai branch from Shri Ramdeen. He is a fine gentleman and was my predecessor as the Head of the Rania branch but now posted as Recovery Officer for many loans sanctioned and disbursed by him have turned sticky."

Ravi Kumar ji continued "Once you have learned all that, you may make me learn how to do all that as I am also not aware of all this. I joined the bank as the Agriculture Field (AFO) and had worked in the advances department all through and the present assignment is the first one to have a head-on interface with routine banking."

I was dumbstruck to listen to such a reply from the Branch Head and wondered which bank I have joined where even Branch Head was not aware of basic banking, so what if he had joined as AFO.

"What a blunder I had made. In the first branch, the Branch Head did not let me learn anything and wasted my time and here in the second branch, the Branch Head himself does not know and is looking forward to me to make him learn." I scratched my hair and cried in the heart of my heart that I had left RBI with grand expectations and here things looked frightening.

I remembered Sengar ji's words again" कहां फंस गए"

All my dreams to make my career after resigning from RBI appeared to have come a cropper.

....AND WE TURNED PARENTS

When I was transferred from Orai to Rania, I started staying at my residence at Souter Ganj. Daily commuting between Kanpur and Rania was a new experience for me. It required leaving home early in the morning and coming back late in the evening. Moreover, the cause of my happiness was that I had learned a lot of banking which I could not in the Orai branch. Soon after joining the Rania branch, Reena informed me with a blush on her face that she was pregnant. It was a matter of extreme happiness for both of us. After all, both of us were going to be parents.

On our first wedding anniversary on 12th March 1987, we went to Yog Restaurant at Moti Jheel. While appreciating the ambience and relishing dinner, we talked to each other. I said to Reena "Next year when we would be celebrating our 2nd marriage anniversary, our baby would be in our laps throwing his or her hand on each item. Just imagine how beautiful that scene would be!"

Reena while listening to this from me expressed her happiness with the shyness of an Indian wife.

But luck was not absolutely with us. A few diagnostic blood tests had revealed Reena as B- whereas I was B+. It is a critical medical problem when a pregnant woman has Rh - factor and her husband Rh + factor. This all results in multiple problems during pregnancy and even the chances of premature delivery are not ruled out. Soon such complications started showing their impact on Reena as well. The first problem arose When she was around five months pregnant and almost reached a stage of premature delivery. Doctors' competence helped save that eventuality. On the doctor's advice bricks were placed under the lower limb side of the bed. Reena remained on high medication and complete bed rest. Reena's position made me feel how risky and painful it was to become a mother.

On the 26th of August 1987 night, Reena was admitted to the hospital and on the 27th morning, a premature but beautiful baby girl was born, and I became a proud papa. My happiness knew no bounds. I had waited in the lawn of the hospital all night for the delivery and my angel came at 6.20 in the morning. This good news was brought to me by Gita. Mami remained in the Labour room all through the night. Reena was extremely happy as she had endured a lot in all these months of pregnancy and finally became a mother. The baby girl was nicknamed Puja by Gita.

Later, Reena named her Sakshi officially. It bears mention that during her days of pregnancy, Reena would often say "if a girl takes birth, I will name her Sakshi and if a boy then Kshitij."

Her contention was that Sakshi means a witness and here Sakshi meant witness to our love. Regarding the name Kshitij she said "Evening" (In Hindi evening means Sandhya, Reena's official name) meets "Sun" (Sun in Hindi means Arun) at Horizon (Kshitij). However, I do not remember why my son was not named Kshitij, instead christened as Shreyansh officially and nicknamed as Shivam by Gita. It is also true that it was me who named him Shreyansh.

Puja was born almost in seven and a half months. Her face was normal but below the shoulder, she was quite weak. Within two days of her birth, she developed juvenile jaundice, a disease quite common in new-born babies. But with serum bilirubin as high as at 12, the hospital doctor made us panicky by suggesting the change of her entire blood. I, Reena, and the entire family got panicky on listening to the talks of the change of blood of a two-day-old premature kid. Anil did not have any kids, we wondered if this baby, who was first between two brothers, would survive or not. Besides, Reena looked worried thinking about what would happen to the baby she had given birth to after undergoing tremendous trauma and pain.

My Mami took her to another child specialist with me who made us comfortable and spoke "There is no need to change the blood as of now the serum bilirubin is not that high to warrant change of blood."

On my query "If the baby needs to be kept in an incubator" he said, "No, not at all! But early in the morning the baby must be kept under sun rays in the bare body for a few minutes and the same thing be repeated in the evening. It should be done at least for five days." He further said, "Sun Rays, particularly in the early morning, have enough Ultraviolet (UV) Rays that help dissolve Serum Bilirubin."

I took responsibility for myself. After all, she was my baby and she had promoted me from a mere husband to a proud Papa.

I did the exercise every morning and evening for more than five days and within a week my angel was fit and fine. After a few days, I got Reena back home.

When Puja was just one month old, she developed a severe cough and cold and was advised of hospitalization. I along with Mami again rushed to the same doctor who simply advised certain antibiotic injections and Puja was fit again. And now my daughter is the mother of a sweet little and naughty baby boy, nicknamed Bunny, aged six plus years.

I wish my darling Puja a healthy long life ahead filled with all happiness along with her husband Pankaj and son Bunny. Tathastu (Amen)....

....And ours became an ideal family

By 1990 Reena had started developing the problem of prolapse whose only solution was the removal of ovaries and the entire uterus. But as the age of Reena was less than 40, doctors said it was against normal medical ethics. The common practice was either the lady was above 40 or had two kids. When Reena's problem refused to subside, we planned our second baby so that we might seek the removal of ovaries and uterus thereafter.

Reena was pregnant again and during pregnancy, she got infected with Hepatitis. Diagnostic results suggested it was Hepatitis B, a serious and contagious disease. Dr Madhu Loomba, under whose supervision Reena was having her treatment, was surprised to know about Reena's Hepatitis B. She did not believe the report.

Dr Loomba said "I cannot believe this report. It cannot be Hepatitis B. It is very uncommon. You get a fresh Test done at Dr Gauri Soor's pathology."

The next report also came as Hepatitis B positive. Dr Loomba got panicky. She called her medical college professor Dr Mittal and said, "Dr I am sending one patient who is pregnant and has tested Hepatitis B positive."

She asked us to visit Dr Mittal at his Medical College campus residence.

Dr Mittal prescribed certain medicines and advised complete bed rest. Oily and rich food was a complete taboo.

He also said," Someone taking care of the patient must get himself vaccinated against Hepatitis B."

As I was the one in close contact with Reena, I got myself vaccinated.

Dr Loomba one day asked me "The case is complicated, and chances of a crunch situation may not be ruled out when we need to go for saving either the mother or the baby. So, take a call in this regard and advise me before delivery."

I immediately said, "Mother. "

After reaching home, Reena cried profusely thinking that she might lose the baby she had been carrying in her womb.

I asked, "Why are you so attached to a baby you haven't seen yet?"

"You males cannot understand the attachment a lady develops with the baby inside her womb the moment she comes to know of conception and now the doctor says to choose between me and my baby How cruel the God is!"

"But that is beyond anybody's control. I pray everything goes well and our baby too gets born healthy." I consoled Reena, hugged her, and brought her close to my heart. She was still sobbing.

Life continued thereafter under the fear of the unknown. somehow Reena could compromise with the unknown fear but prayed daily for the best. By God's grace, Reena turned Hepatitis B negative a few weeks before the expected delivery date. The God almighty had listened to our prayers, especially Reena's. She had a sigh of relief and started having positive vibes.

On 6th July 1991, I went to Lucknow in connection with the marriage of a friend.

I asked Gita to come and stay at my place with Reena so that in case of any emergency she could be of help to Reena.

On the 7th morning at about 7 AM, Reena started developing labour pains and Gita rushed her to the hospital on a cycle rickshaw. When she reached the hospital, one lady Dr Mishra was at the gate to take a rickshaw back home. As Dr Mishra was known to Gita, so on her request she stayed back and took Reena to the labour room. Soon thereafter, a baby boy was born.

I came back in the afternoon from Lucknow and found the house locked. I was told by the neighbourhood that Reena was hospitalized and had delivered a baby boy in the morning. I was on cloud nine as the baby who was not expected to get birth was born safely. I kept my bag there and rushed towards the hospital on a cycle rickshaw as my scooter was in the locked house. That day the distance between Souter Ganj and Dufferin hospital at Bada chauraha appeared too long and I kept pushing the Rickshaw puller to run faster. Each passing second and minute looked like years and was making me restless.

On reaching the hospital room, I saw a little baby lying on the bed beside Reena. After seeing me Reena, not only had a sigh of relief but also a satisfying and blushing smile. My son was sleeping in a white vest and langoti (Homemade diaper).

We were happy that the baby whose survival was doubtful was born safe and healthy.

Mine was an ideal family now consisting of five...Amma, me, Reena, Puja, and the newly arrived son. I thanked God for what he had done for us. My son Shivam is now a Cinematographer, Director and editor and based in Mumbai. I wish him all success and a long and healthy life ahead. Tathastu...(Amen)

I would be interested to narrate an innocent story here. One day when Reena was still in the hospital, Puja was home with me and

Amma. While lying on the bed she looked at me and very innocently asked me "पापा ये बेबी आपको क्या कहेगा?" (Papa what this baby would call you?)

I instantly replied "ये भी आपकी तरह पापा कहेगा?" (Like you, he would also call me Papa)

It looked like my reply was a shocker for Puja. A nonplussed Puja rolled her eyes and after a pause said, "पापा अगर ये बेबी आपको पापा कहेगा तो मैं आपको चाचा कहूंगी" (Papa if the baby would call you Papa, then I would call you Chacha)."

I was astounded to hear such a reply from Puja who was less than four years old.

I could sense the dilemma she was in and the uneasiness she was going through. I realized that so far, there was none except her only to call me Papa.

My nieces- Sheebu, Shilpi and Khushboo had been calling me Mama only. Comprehending the tender emotions and feelings of Puja's innocent heart, I immediately rolled back my words and said, "आप क्यों चाचा कहोगी? ये बेबी मुझे चाचा कहेगा और सिर्फ आप पापा कहोगी" (Why would you call me chacha. This little baby would call me Chacha and you only would say, Papa)

Puja's eyes gleamed with happiness, she smiled, got up from the bed, jumped up and hugged me by coming in my lap, shouting "मेरे पापा सबसे अच्छे" (my father is the best).

Later, I tried to analyse the innocence of a kid's heart. I realized that kids are too possessive about their parents and cannot share their love and affection with anyone. Puja being a daughter was too attached to me and after a single-child journey of almost four years, she was not ready to share her Papa with the little baby boy who had just arrived a couple of days back.

It is otherwise that Puja now loves that baby boy trillions like her own little son Bunny officially called Shaurya. May this continue forever...

I must say it was innocence at its height and Puja personified Innocence.

Almost near to putting in my papers

In June 1997 I got promoted to scale II and the designated place of posting was Kamasin district Banda. It was amongst the worst branches of the Hamirpur region of the bank. I was to join on 16th June 1997. Prior to that, I met my Zonal Head and requested him to change my posting to some convenient place which he flatly refused.

The day of joining was fast approaching. I had to go alone initially and then my family was to reach there. Three or four days before my leaving, I got very nervous. The little Puja, seeing me nervous, tried her best to boost my morale and said "Papa look, Salil uncle has also lived alone in Orai for two years, you can also stay there. Come on Papa."

All this morale-boosting notwithstanding, I even started thinking of quitting the bank and starting giving tuition. I had discussions with a friend who was giving tuition.

The next day Reena said, "last night I had a dream which broke my sleep and I got panicky."

She continued "I saw a lady begging in the street with her small kids, one girl and one boy and It appeared to me as if it was me with Puja and Shivam"

On my questioning as to why she felt so after the dream, she started sobbing "Your idea of quitting the job and starting tuition frightened me so much that I could identify myself with that lady."

I had understood what point Reena was trying to drive home. She in fact wanted me to continue with the bank and join the Kamasin branch. She then openly said, "For the sake of my kids, please do not resign and continue with the bank. Go there, find a house, and soon I along with Amma and kids will join you there." Reena had opened my eyes and I dropped the idea of quitting the bank.

I still do not know if what Reena told me was a real dream or just a story to make me realize the reality of life and quit the idea of resigning from the bank.

I left for Kamasin on the 16th of June 1997 morning by bus and reached Banda. I headed towards Tulsi lodge where a few friends of mine were also residing and I too had to stay till I found the house. After dropping my goods there in the lodge, I left for Kamasin by a private bus and reported for duty in the afternoon.

One, Mishraji, father-in-law of Manish, our jijaji's cousin, was of immense help and guidance in Banda. I and Reena addressed him as Papa. He arranged a free monthly bus pass for commuting between Banda to Kamasin and back. He was like our guardian there. His entire family was wonderful, especially his son Atul and daughter Archana. Mishraji helped me find a house in another block of the colony where his residence was. After I had searched the house, I came to Kanpur to take Amma, Reena, and kids to Banda. Jijaji accompanied us to Banda and stayed with us for a week.

One Shri Chunnoo Singh, Development Officer in an Insurance company was another person who helped us beyond our imagination. He was there in our thick and thin like Papa. One Shri Santosh Mishra, a clerk in our Banda branch was another helping hand and would often visit our residence.

Once I was returning from Kamasin to Banda by bus. It had rained heavily before. The soil of Banda was such as roads had become too slippery. Roads were narrow and suddenly one bus skidded, and the entire traffic was blocked. The buses on the other side were returning to Banda but it was not possible to come over to the other side. People said to me that there was no need to panic as soon everything would be alright. I stayed put in the bus. After half an hour I started getting panicky as it looked like it was difficult to reach home tonight.

I asked the conductor of a solo bus, all other buses had already returned, on the opposite side "Turn back and take us to Banda"

He said, "Fork out Rs. 300 upfront." I asked many people to contribute but no one came forward.

As the time was running fast and it was sunset, I thought "If I fail to reach home tonight my family would be worrying too much about my whereabouts."

I continued thinking "Arun nothing is more important than the peace and happiness of the family. So, give Rs. 300 to the conductor and reach home."

I forked out Rs. 300 from my pocket and asked the conductor to start for the Banda. The driver turned back and I boarded the bus. The moment I boarded; a swarm of people tried to board as well. An infuriated me stood at the entry of the bus and denied free entry to all and said "If anyone is willing to go to Banda give upfront Rs. 20 or I am going alone on this bus."

After some altercations, people started forking out Rs. 20 each and this way I collected Rs. 240 and my stake now was reduced only to Rs. 60.

Thus, I reached home by 10 PM and found my family standing at the gate of the house. My arrival comforted their hearts and my kids, Puja and Shivam jumped up and Shivam came in my lap.

Today I feel if only Mobile telephony was as readily available as it is today, such a situation could have been managed in a better way.

The next day when I was coming back to the office by another bus, the conductor of the bus said to me "Last night someone brought back an entire bus on his own by paying Rs. 300."

When I asked him "Do you know who that person was,"

He said "No."

I Said that "That person is in front of you."

He looked at me with awe and said "Oh!"

SHIVAM FALLING SICK

By September 2004, I was transferred from the Zonal office, Hamirpur to Kanpur FIO. On 13th September I reported for duty as senior Vigilance officer. I was literally under the control of the Head Office. My leave would get sanctioned by The Chief Vigilance Officer (CVO) at HO and I would get me my investigative assignments from HO.

Once I went to Varanasi zone for investigation and on the day, I was supposed to leave for Kanpur by night train, I got a call on my mobile in the afternoon from Reena speaking in a trembling voice "Come back to Kanpur immediately as Shivam has got a massive fit and has been taken to Hospital by Isaac Bhaiya." Mr. Issac was our neighbour.

I was shocked and frightened as well. I said, "Ok do not worry, I am coming."

Then I called Issac Bhaiya who was our wonderful friend and always ready to help. He was my age "Issac Bhai," what has happened to Shivam?"

"Nothing to worry dear. He had a fit and his CT scan has been done. Doctors say it is because of a cyst." Issac Bhai said.

I handed over my 2nd AC ticket to Ravi Srivastava, my ex-colleague at Kanpur and currently posted at Varanasi for cancellation. He arranged a 2nd class ordinary ticket but I boarded the 2nd AC coach of the train.

As expected, the Travelling Ticket Inspector (TTI) came and asked for the ticket. I took the ordinary ticket out and gave it to him.

"It is an ordinary 2nd class ticket and you are in the 2nd AC compartment. You need to pay the penalty." TTI told me.

"Yes, I know it is an ordinary 2nd class ticket. I had reservation in another night train in 2nd AC but as my son has fallen sick suddenly, I am running back in an emergency. Anyways, please let me know how much penalty is to be paid for continuing my journey till Kanpur." I replied in a sad and worried manner.

TTI looked at me with his eyes expressing compassion for me. He said "Ok, continue your journey. I pray your son recovers soon." TTI went off without asking for any money or penalty.

One nearby passenger who was all ears to this discussion asked me very politely "Please share the berth with me till Kanpur. I will sleep thereafter as I am booked for New Delhi." The passenger was so kind that he shared his food with me also. He also enquired as to what had happened to my son.

The train was moving towards Kanpur and the journey looked too long. The fear of the unknown was hitting hard. During that period Reena did not own a mobile phone, so it was a contactless journey. The train reached Kanpur and I took leave of the Passenger by shaking hands and conveying my sincere thanks. I also thanked TTI who too had come before I deboarded. Both waved their hands and wished my son a quick recovery and good health.

Really there is no dearth of good people around us.

It was around 2.30 AM when I reached home. As it was already too late, I thought Shivam might be sleeping. So, I stayed back at home and reached Hospital early in the morning and saw Shivam lying on the bed and Reena sitting beside him. Both looked relaxed after seeing me.

"What happened beta? I asked Shivam.

He simply smiled a bit and expressed his ignorance about what had happened to him. Reena told me "Doctors say it is because of a cyst and is curable. It is not risky."

I met Doctors who advised, "There is nothing to worry about as this is a very common problem, particularly in kids, caused by eating pork or cauliflower."

The doctor continued "Black spots on the leaves of cauliflower generally carry cysts and when they somehow get into blood capillaries of the brain, this causes fits to happen. This disease is called Neurocysticercosis. My advice to all is not to consume cauliflower with spotted leaves and avoid pork as well. The treatment is simple but lengthy where medicines must be taken religiously without fail as any break in medication, if followed by a fit, would mean to start the treatment afresh."

I had a sigh of relief after having words with the doctor.

Later, I was told that after coming from school Shivam was lying on the double bed with Amma and suddenly Amma felt Shivam's hand on her back. Thinking Shivam was deliberately playing pranks, Amma kept mum and when Shivam's hand remained on her back, she turned only to find froth coming out of Shivam's mouth and he was unconscious. Amma shouted and Reena and Puja rushed from another room. Our neighbour Shri Issac was called, and he brought Shivam down from the first floor and rushed away to nearby Bhargav Hospital.

Shivam was brought back from the Hospital in a couple of days with instructions to continue medication religiously. We then consulted a neuro physician named Dr Vikas Dixit and he had been instrumental in Shivam's successful treatment. My sincere thanks to Dr Dixit.

After a week, Shivam had yet another fit and this time his jaw got a little twisted and his voice also turned a little less comprehensible.

Dr Dixit was on contact advised that in the initial days, some more fits could not be ruled out and it was a normal phenomenon.

It would be worth mentioning here that Shivam had been very cooperative during his medication and took medicines religiously without a single break. By the mid of 2008, Shivam was alright and by God's grace and blessings he is absolutely fit. May he live a long and healthy life always. Tathastu (Amen)...

AFTER 25 LONG YEARS

It was perhaps June 2007, when Kavita Rohatgi, a classmate of mine and Deepika in M.Sc., who was married in 1982 and settled in Mumbai, came to Kanpur in connection with her bank training at Lucknow. She was in the United Bank of India (now merged with Punjab National Bank). Before going back to Mumbai, she one day asked me to call on her. Her maternal home was nearby mine. I went there to see her.

I knew Kavita would be in touch with Deepika, so after discussing other things, I asked her "Where is She?'

"Who?" she questioned.

"Oh, yaar, I am talking about Deepika."

"She got been married in 1986. Initially, she was in Allahabad and now has shifted to New Delhi."

"Give me her mobile number," I spoke

"I do not have one right now." She spoke.

"Yaar it would be in your mobile contact list."

"No yaar this is the different mobile set, and the number is in another set that is in Mumbai right now." She spoke again.

I knew she was not wanting to share her number with me and that is why she was lying.

"Fine, when you talk to her next time, give her my number and if she would consider it fit, she would make a call." I finally said.

I came back home thinking Kavita had avoided giving me Deepika's number fearing I might call her thereby some creating probable trouble.

A few days thereafter, Kavita called me "I gave her your number. She talked to her husband about talking to you but her husband was not in favour of her calling you."

"Ok, no issues. Kavita. I do not know if her husband is right or wrong, but certainly, he appears to be very conservative and does not let his wife talk to her college friend." I replied frustratedly.

"Arun, Deepika had earlier told him about her college life relationship with you and that is why he has denied her talking to you apprehending the revival of old flames within both of you which might not be in the interest of your and her family," Kavita told

I replied to Kavita "Anyways it was her choice to abide by her husband's suggestions."

It was sometime in September 2007, and I got a call in the evening while I was home. A female was on the other side saying "Hello Arun."

The voice and style appeared quite familiar but I asked, "who is on the line, please?"

The Female voice said something which I could not hear.

"Pardon, I could not hear?" I replied.

"It is me, Deepika. How are you?" she said.

"Oh my God! It is you, Deepika. I cannot believe it." I was on cloud nine finding her on the line.

"But Kavita told me that your husband has denied you talking to me" I quipped.

"Yes, he did. But after getting your number from Kavita, I could not hold myself back. He is not aware of this call." She spoke.

"How is everyone in your family? How are Aunty, Reena, Puja, and Shivam?" She asked.

"Oh, you know everyone in my family. I think you got the information from Kavita. Anyways, we all are fine. What about you and your family." I asked

"Yes, Kavita told me about your family. By the way, I am fine. My husband is Rakesh and a CA by profession. We have two sons. One is studying engineering and the other is in college." She replied

"That's good," I said.

We talked about a lot of things and went down memory lane as well but neither she nor I talked about the 1983 episode.

"One thing Arun. Please do not call from your side. I will call you when I find the time." She spoke before putting down the phone.

Finding me unusually happy after the call, Reena asked me "Looking very happy. Whose call was this?"

An honest me could not lie to Reena and frankly said "Deepika."

"Deepika! How come Deepika called you after so many years? She questioned.

"I do not know. But I had asked Kavita to give my number to her." I said straight from the heart, without concealing anything.

"But why, in the first place, did you ask Kavita to give your number? It means you wanted to talk to her?" She fired the gun.

"Come on, you are unnecessarily raising an alarm. While I met Kavita recently, we discussed about our friends including Deepika and then I asked her to give my number to Deepika. Be a sport Reena. We were friends and a reunion with her is not bad either.

Moreover, she is married and has two grown-up kids like us." I said to her,

"I am not raising any alarm but as a wife not finding all this palatable." She protested.

"Look Reena, had there been any sort of otherwise intention, I would have not told you it was Deepika. I could have taken some other name. So, if you cannot trust me, trust my honesty." I made a strong point.

Reena had no reply and just spoke smilingly "Would you like to have a cup of tea?

"Why not, better if with some hot pakoras." I replied with joy, sensing Reena had got my point correctly.

Thereafter, calls from her kept coming very occasionally and I never concealed it from Reena.

In the first week of June 2008, Deepika gave me a call and advised she was coming to Kanpur and wanted to meet me. We fixed the meeting on 11th June just because exactly twenty-five years back we had met last at her residence when I visited with a marriage proposal. The meeting place fixed was Arya Nagar where one of her friends resided.

I took leave on that date from the office. As usual, I did not keep things secret from Reena and even advised her that Deepika would come home to see you. Reena's body language looked against what I had planned.

I reached the rendezvous on time in my Sunday best. She came with her friend and introduced her to me and thereafter her friend moved away.

There was now none barring her and me. I took her to my Maruti 800 Non-AC car parked a short distance away. It was an extremely hot noon and my locked car had become a gas chamber. The chocolates bought for her had melted and the rose wilted.

"Sorry yaar, it is too hot here in the car. It looks like a hot furnace." I turned apologetic.

She smiled and said "No issues. It is ok."

The moment my car picked up speed, she asked the first but expected question "Why did you not wait for me when you came to my house with a proposal in 1983 and left without meeting me?"

"Honestly speaking that day Aunty's behaviour compelled me to think that you had played a double game with me," I replied

"What! Double game! Arun, it has been your habit to jump to conclusions too soon. how could you derive that conclusion?" she asked.

"Deepu, my asking the straight question of marrying you was expected to raise Aunty's eye brows but contrary to it she responded very calmly. She did not lose her temper. I had been under the impression that she would certainly take my coming up with a proposal very seriously. I was pretty sure that she would scold me. But Aunty was as cold as ice and such behaviour was contrary to what I had imagined" I spoke.

"My mummy did not say harsh words to you...remained calm and you inferred I played a game, a double game. Did you come to my house with the impression that you would get a beating and some rowdy scenes happen? How foolish of you Arun?" she said.

I replied "Deepika, I do not know if I am right or wrong, but I am sure anyone under that circumstances must have thought that way. Aunty's such calm, cool and icy behaviour left me with no option but to think that you certainly had advised Aunty to play cool with me. Deny the relationship on the caste basis. This way, I think, you thought neither Aunty had to be rough with me nor I would feel insulted and go back."

"It attests that your claim that you understood me inside out was an absolute lie. Arun, after that phone call I got involved in making tea and snacks and it obviously took some time and when I came back with refreshments, I saw you were not there. I asked mummy about you and I was told you have already gone. And when I asked mummy what happened then she told me everything." She spoke.

"You will not believe Arun; I cried profusely that night in isolation fearing it was our last meeting." She added.

Going ahead she said "After that incident, I was not allowed to move alone. My Papa got angry not only at me but uttered some rough words about you as well. He was so furious that he even told my brothers to bring you before him so that you might be given a lesson but I could, somehow, rein in my brothers."

She did not stop here and said "You will not believe I made all out efforts to trace you but could not. Every time I visited Navin Market, I hoped against hope of meeting you. Despite knowing your address, I could not come to you. Arun, I even thought of not marrying anyone else after that incident. But one day I was shocked when I got your marriage card through Hemant. I thought how come you could marry a girl other than me? Was your love for me so superficial? Without meeting me one more time you had decided to marry and even dared send your marriage card to me.

Arun that night I passed crying all through. And, then only, I decided to marry myself. Arun, you do not know, the day you tied the knot with Reena, I was having my Ring ceremony celebrations."

I was shocked at such a revelation.

"Arun, though it is irrelevant now, tell me why you gave up and did not try once more? It seems you came to my place just for the sake of formality." She had put my love for her on scrutiny.

"Now what should I say? Yes, I must have attempted once more. Anyways, Deepu, both of us are now happy with our spouses and love them too much. We have our families now, so better, let the bygones be bygones. Despite being the first love of each other, we now can be best friends forever." I spoke.

"Of course, I am happy with Rakesh and you with Reena. They all love us beyond measure but after meeting you today all those emotions have just surfaced again. Ok, I agree with you to let the past be buried and we remain eternal friends and let our love remain the platonic love." She spoke with her signature smile.

Thereafter I took out the birthday and new year greeting cards as well as friendly letters sent by her during college days from the bag.

She wondered "Oh my God! You have kept all these so securely, I cannot believe it."

She read a few of the letters and looked at me and blushed.

We had reached my residence by now. I rang the bell and it was none other than Reena who opened the door. Both looked at each other for a moment and then hugged each other.

Reena led her to the living room. After the exchange of pleasantries, Reena asked her bluntly "Deepika when both of you loved each other, why did you two not get married?"

I was expecting this query from Reena but it would be so direct I had not thought of.

Deepika looked at me and smiled away without giving any answer.

After half an hour, Deepika wanted to visit Navin Market to purchase certain things for my kids. Reena too wanted to come along but I said: "Reena you stay back, I just come back." Reena did not like it and went upstairs. Later I realized that it was a blunder on my part. I must have taken her along with us.

Thereafter, I dropped Deepika at her residence and when I took leave, she extended her hand for a handshake and this took me unawares as in college we had never touched each other. I had my maiden Handshake with her on that day. She appeared to have become more modern by staying in New Delhi.

Two days later we met again at Café Coffee Day and enjoyed a cup of coffee. Here while discussing over a cup of Coffee, she asked me about a mathematical puzzle which I failed to solve and said "Sorry, I give up."

"Arun, as usual you have given up early. You had earlier given up in 1983 as well, you remember." She sarcastically chuckled.

I had no words but hushed up the issue with a fake smile "Yaar, do not talk of 1983. It has gone into history, and I think none of us has ever been a student of history."

Two or three days thereafter, she left Kanpur for Delhi and sent me various messages. In one message she wrote, "My Kanpur visit post marriage has never been so satisfying."

A few months later she again visited Kanpur. This time she visited my house with her husband. We had a gala time together.

Over the period, the frequency of calls increased from both sides. And this made Reena occasionally ask me why I did not marry Deepika when I loved her too much. This question often made me feel Reena had a sense of infidelity from my side. There was no denying that Deepika was my first love and no one forgets the first love. But it was a fact that now Reena was not only my wife but my love as well. I tried to convince Reena that Deepika had been in my life prior to her coming into my life. So, by any reckoning, it was not a case of an extramarital relationship. It was rather a case of two old friends, who once had been in love and could not get into a relationship, coming back in contact again and hence there was no reason to suspect anything. I had failed to convince Reena that after meeting with Deepika the resurfacing of old emotions was a normal phenomenon. Simultaneously I had also failed to realize that no wife would tolerate her husband talking to a lady friend, particularly when the two have had some affair between them earlier. Though I and Reena loved each other too much and our relationship never got sour, I could see the random pain in Reena's eyes sporadically. I feel sorry that I could not satisfy her intermittent restlessness. I, at times, feel guilty, not because I at all had cheated her but because I failed to clear her doubts about my relationship with Deepika.

Later, both, I and Deepika decided to do something so that neither it created any sort of wrong impression about our present relationship in the minds of our spouses nor it precipitated into any unpleasant situation. As a result, calls from both the sides started getting reduced and ultimately turned into a once in blue affair that too to get to know about each other's welfare only.

PUJA LEAVES FOR HIGHER STUDIES & MY PROMOTION

In 2009 Puja had to join the Institute of Management & Research (IMDR) Pune to do her Post Graduate Diploma in Management. The mere thought of her leaving home and going alone to Pune was simply killing me. I would not be able to sleep properly and often get up in the wee hours of the morning and start roaming here and there. Reena was worried about my condition. Nothing was soothing to me. My friends, who would travel with me to Lucknow daily, also tried to comfort me and gave their examples, but nothing could help me. I would often go to Puja at night to see if she was sleeping or worried like me.

Then came the day when we all had to leave for Pune to drop her at Pune. On reaching Pune I, Reena, Puja, and Shivam stayed with Ashish, Jijaji's nephew. On the next day, we went to see Puja's Paying Guest (PG) hostel and then came back. I also left Puja at PG for a day while we were in Pune to see if she could live without us.

Now the day of our departure had arrived. I said "Beta! Now we will take your leave."

Lo and behold, Puja burst into a huge cry, and it made me further weak. I immediately asked, "Repack your goods and return to Kanpur with us. You will study further there only."

"No Papa, I will study here." She spoke.

"Why did you cry then?" I asked her.

"It was just an emotional outburst Papa as I was going to live without you all. I am ok now." She stated and put on a plastic smile.

"Ok then, we leave" we left her PG with a heavy heart by the taxi we have hired for Kalyan to catch the train therefrom for Kanpur. I saw Puja's eyes strolling us till she could see us.

Reena had almost travelled back to Kanpur with her eyes filled with tears.

On 8th December 2009, I was promoted to the next level but the posting had not come yet. The news of the transfer came to me on 24th December 2009

I was relieved from FIO on 22nd January 2010 only to report at the Nehru Colony branch, Dehradun on 25th.

It was 23rd January 2010. I had to catch Sangam Express which starts from Prayagraj (Then Allahabad) and reaches Kanpur at 9.25 PM. Those were densely foggy days and nights, and trains had been running late. I left home in Anil's car accompanied by Bhabhi, Jijaji and Reena. It was too foggy, and visibility was almost Zero. Somehow, we reached the station. Anil and Bhabhi went off by dropping us at Station. Jijaji and Reena accompanied me inside the station. Train, as expected, was late and arrived at 11 PM. I boarded the train with a heavy heart as I was leaving my family knowing that my family would come only after Shivam's 12th Standard papers were over. The train whistled and started crawling slowly. I, while standing at the gate of the train, waved to Reena and Jijaji with tears in my eyes. Reena too looked gloomy and waved back to me.

An old lady wanted me to exchange her upper berth with my lower one and without a second thought I acceded to her request.

She thanked me and I smiled back only as if I was saying we must have respect and care for elders. I retired myself on upper birth, calling a few friends, as also to Reena.

By the next morning, the train got further delayed. In my opposite berth was one Sardarji, Shri Chaddha who was traveling with his wife. Talks revealed that he was a retired officer from IFFCO. He was also going to Dehradun where he had his flat. On knowing that I was Chief Manager of Allahabad Bank and going to join Nehru Colony, he said it was close to his residence. He enquired about my staying arrangements at Dehradun.

The train got further delayed and Chadhaji started saying "Stay with us tonight and tomorrow I will drop you at your branch."

I refused but he and his wife prevailed upon me. The train reached Dehradun at 9 PM against the normal time of 1 PM at noon.

We all reached Chaddha ji's house and therefrom to his brother's house for dinner. The Chaddhas were a wonderfully helping family. After dinner, we went back to Chaddha ji's flat. Chaddha ji had no kids. He lived in his flat with his wife only.

The next day I had breakfast at his flat. As I had to go back to Lucknow in the evening for a CBI court case whose investigation was done by me, I left my bag with Chaddha ji. I came to the branch with Chadhaji. He introduced me to the branch staff saying "He is Mr. Misra, your Branch Head. We have come together and he stayed with me last night. Now take care of him."

The same evening, I boarded a train for Lucknow. After attending court and making a day's visit to Kanpur also, I had returned to Dehradun by bus.

On reaching back, Chadhaji was all help again and got me a good hotel at very subsidised rates. We maintained good relations with Chaddha ji's family. Really, good people are there in this world who make it worth living.

One day Shri Nathi Ram, senior Manager at our bank's Roorkee branch came to my branch and enquired about my staying arrangement. I asked him "Find one self-contained room. Right now, I am in a hotel."

"Ok, I see to it." Nath Ram said and moved away.

After one hour Nathi Ram returned and took me to a house just behind the branch where on the 2nd floor there was a room with attached toilet and bathroom. It was good, giving a beautiful panoramic view of the Mall Road of Mussoorie. I came to know it was Nathi Ram's own house and perhaps he wanted to discuss it with his wife before saying yes to me and that was why he initially did not tell me. Nathi Ram ji, Bhabhi ji and the kids were very helpful people.

I stayed there comfortably for almost four months and in the interim, I had found one complete 2 BHK independent residence just two houses away from my current place. The agreement for the lease was done. I went to Kanpur in May and brought Amma, Reena and Shivam by a hired Jeep and goods by truck.

The entire stay at Dehradun was fine where I made good relations with Rajan Pundir, S.N. Dobhal, Anil Mittal, B.S. Rawat, Rama Nigam, B.S Romar, Harish Mehta, Umrao singh, Rakesh Jain, Anil Gupta, Shivani etc.

My Zonal Head Mr. M.S. Ojha was very gentle and always very supportive. His wife had very good relations with Reena.

SHIVAM LEAVES FOR HIGHER STUDIES, PUJA'S MARRIAGE & BUNNY'S BIRTH

In 2010, during my posting at Dehradun, Shivam started taking coaching for Engineering Competitive examinations at Akash Institute. He took a couple of engineering tests and was allotted some colleges including the University of Petroleum and Energy Studies (UPES), Dehradun. But he preferred to do Sound Engineering from a private college in Mumbai. It was a course, at least, I was unaware of. I was in a fix. I asked my Bhabhi, who was a teacher in Kanpur, to enquire about the course from the sources she had. She talked with certain people and came up with positive opinions.

Meanwhile, I learned that one of my bank clients, Dr Kamal Bansal, was a professor at UPES and, thankfully, lived in the Nehru colony, where I also lived.

"Sir, this is my son and has been picked for B. Tech from your University but he does not want to complete standard engineering courses, rather wants to join Sound Engineering from a private college in Mumbai," I told Dr Bansal one day when I visited his residence with my son.

“I am not sure whether I should let him pursue his goal or enrol him in your university. Please advise me on what to do." I asked further.

“Misraji, doing engineering from my university means, he will become a man of minimum Rs. 40 K per month but where he wants to go means he may take you either to the sky or bring you down to the Floor. Anyways, let me have a one-on-one interaction with him.” Dr Bansal spoke to me.

"Sure, Sir. You may talk to him." I replied and then asked Shivam to go inside with Dr Bansal.

Dr Bansal and Shivam went inside and I kept sitting in the living room.

After 15 minutes or so, both came back and Dr Bansal asked Shivam to walk on the lawn outside. Off went Shivam and Dr Bansal spoke to me "Misraji, let this boy fly his wings. He has ample fire in his belly for pursuing his passion. I asked him some academic and some unrelated questions and the way he replied was simply awesome. The sky's the limit for this boy."

I was happy that my confusion was almost over.

I came back home with Shivam and at night told Reena everything about my meeting with Dr Bansal. I spoke to her "Let Shivam pursue his passion. I could not do what I wanted in my life because Pitaji did not permit me to follow my passion for singing and after his demise, there was none to stand by me in taking the risk that was inherent in pursuing my dream and afford the bill, of course. As I am alive, I do not want my son to let his passion die for any reason. So, for me, he is going to Mumbai. What is your take?'

"What I can say is if you feel it is good, it is good for me as well. I stand by your decision." Reena replied as a typical middle-class wife and mother.

Tickets for Mumbai were booked and I along with Reena and Shivam flew to Mumbai. Puja was already there in Mumbai as she had been working with Hindustan Pencils Ltd after PGDM and staying in a PG at Colaba. She also joined us. We visited Shivam's college the next day and searched PGs for Shivam's stay.

One PG was finalised in Andheri (West) close to Shivam's college. Then arrived the day of taking leave of Shivam. I reached Mumbai Airport with Reena, Puja, and Shivam.

When the time to enter the airport came, both Puja and Shivam booked a Taxi for going back. Puja boarded first and Shivam thereafter., To my utter surprise, when Shivam boarded, he saw Puja sobbing. He asked Puja "Why are you crying? You are already away from Mummy and Papa and It is me who is getting away from them today for the first time. So, if anybody is to cry it should be me,"

I was surprised that a boy in his teens, who was going to live away from his parents for the first time, was so bold and strong.

Off went their Taxi and I and Reena entered the airport building with a heavy heart as now we were going to live without both our kids.

While we had boarded the plane, I saw a post on Shivam's Facebook wall "Mummy n Papa Went back. My hostel life starts now. Love you Papa Mummy. Take care."

Though this message had nothing special but the words did speak that Shivam was sad from within but he did not bring it on his face. His message was also loudly speaking about love and concern for us which he never expressed overtly. Shivam still carries such qualities.

During our stay at Dehradun, Reena had started thinking about Puja's marriage as she had completed her PGDM and was in a job as well. I would often ask Puja if she had any liking for any boy, she could very candidly tell me. Puja had always denied it. However, later Puja told us about a boy who had been with her in the PGDM course. The name of the boy was Pankaj Singh who hailed from Patna. It was an inter-caste relation as Pankaj was a Thakur by caste and it gave initial jerks to Reena who was a bit conservative. However, soon she could reconcile herself, of course, after my counselling. Then it was decided to go to Patna to meet the parents of Pankaj. But luck had something else in the store, I got my left hand, my working hand, fractured which made me incapable of undertaking a long journey to Patna. Later, after my plaster was cut, we discussed with Pankaj's family if they could come over to New Delhi, close to Dehradun, for the discussion. A gentle family as they were, they acceded to our request, and we assembled in New Delhi. On my side Amma, Anil, Bhabhi, Gita and Jijaji whereas on Pankaj's side his entire family including his Dadi, Papa, Mummy, Brothers, Sisters, and Brother-in-law were present.

After a short discussion, the marriage was finalised, and I threw a small party in a restaurant. Pankaj's Dadi gave Puja Rs. 5 K. Later, the Ring Ceremony was celebrated at a Hotel in Patna on 23rd November 2012. The closest of my relatives attended the party.

Marriage was celebrated on 27th January 2013 at Kanpur attended by about 500 persons from our side besides a Barat of about 50 persons. It was organised in a beautifully decorated Pandal at Ved Guest House. All rituals were completed without any hassle. The next morning Vidayee was done, and Puja left with Pankaj and family by train.

While going back, Pankaj sent me a WhatsApp message "Papa, I challenge you that I would give your daughter more love and care than you have given her so far."

It was a very soothing message and I was assured that my daughter had selected the right life partner. It brought tears of joy to my eyes. On 30th January 2013, a reception party was thrown by Pankaj's family at Patna which was attended by me, Reena, and Shivam only from my side.

A few months after marriage, Puja resigned from her job and went to Bhandara, near Nagpur where Pankaj was posted.

From Dehradun, I was transferred in August, 2013 to Meerut and posted at the Zonal Office. After two years, I got to know about Puja's pregnancy. Puja had by now shifted to Hinghan Ghat District Wardha with the transfer of Pankaj. Puja was expected to bear a baby by March 2016. In November 2015, I along with Reena went to Hinghan Ghat. I stayed there for a week and came back to Meerut but Reena stayed there for another 50 or so days to help Puja in her tough days of pregnancy. Almost after 50 days, Reena came back to Meerut when Puja's mother-in-law had reached there. She remained there till Puja's pregnancy and thereafter as well. In the third week of March, Reena went there again to help Puja and her mother-in-law in Puja's prenatal and postnatal days. On the 20th Morning at about 4 AM, I got a call from Reena "You have become Nana and I Nani (Grandfather and Grandmother)."

It was a wonderful feeling which was an encore of the feeling I have had when Puja and Shivam were born. It was a moment of extreme joy for us as this was the first baby to have come in my family after Shivam. On reaching the office I asked peon to bring sweets for the entire office.

The Bunny is now a cute little boy of six plus years. After the birth of Puja and Shivam, Amma used to repeat a saying very often that

'मूल से सूद ज्यादा प्यारा होता है (The interest is always sweeter than the principal). She would mean that my kids, Puja and Shivam (Interest) were more adorable to her than her own, that is me (Principal). I found Amma absolutely correct after Bunny's entry in our family. Really, I wish Bunny a long healthy life and may all his dreams come true. Tathastu (Amen).

It would not be proper if I do not narrate one funny incident that happened one night while I was in office. I received a telephone call from Reena at about 9 pm. She asked "where are you?"

"Of course, in the office," I replied.

"So late?" Reena questioned.

"Our bank is going through a lean phase so we are sitting late and working hard to promote and save the bank," I replied jokingly.

"Wow, a man who could not promote himself is promoting his bank. Great. Better be home soon." Reena replied sarcastically.

It was a fact that in the last promotion result declared recently, I could not make it to the list of successful candidates. The reply of Reena had made me ponder if she had been smacking my incapability to get promoted or tangentially hitting the bank for failing to recognise my calibre and competence. This incident gave me a thread to post a sarcastic satire on Facebook which was read, enjoyed, and commented upon by many.

AMMA BHI CHALI GAYI

While Reena was in Hinghan Ghat, one day Anil informed me that Amma had slipped and broken her hip joint. She was scheduled to be put under the knife on the 17th of March. I told Anil that I was coming to Kanpur, but he prevented me. Gita had not been advised of the incident by Anil so I informed not only to Gita but Reena also who was in Hinghan Ghat with Puja. Amma's operation was said to be successful.

A few days after the surgery, I got a call from Bhabhi advising me of Amma developing a Hematoma. Her position was reported to be critical. A surgery was to be performed but doctors were reluctant to do surgery vis a vis Amma's age. I wanted to come down to Kanpur but Bhabhi asked me to wait for a day. I still remember that night I cried like a kid and prayed to God to save my Amma. I loved Amma too much and just because of her I did not take the job of PO in SBBJ in 1985. I remember that on that night my Zonal Head Dr D.P. Singh, who is unfortunately no more with us, on coming to know about my situation offered all moral support to me. May his soul rest in peace

The next day I contacted Bhabhi and was informed that Amma was better now. A couple of days after, the Holi holidays were in the offing. I booked tickets and reached Kanpur. By now Doctors had taken a bold call to go for surgery. Though the surgery was reported to be alright, I remember Amma did not recover.

I informed Reena of all these developments, and she found herself in a catch-22 situation, neither in a position to leave Puja nor in a position to come to Kanpur to take care of Amma. A few days later, I went back to Meerut.

In the meantime, I got information about my transfer to Mumbai circle. I was to join Gandhi Dham (Gujrat), near the western coastal border of India.

On 29th April 2016, I called my FGM and requested "Sir, my mother is critically ill. So, please retain me in Meerut for two months only as within that period my mother will either recover or move to her ultimate destination. The posting of Gandhi Dham is too far off and if anything happens to my mother, I may not get a chance to see her before cremation."

"Do not say such an inauspicious thing. Anyways, send a representation mediately." FGM sir told me. I sent my representation duly recommended by my Zonal Head, Mr. D.P. Singh.

In the evening, FGM sir called and informed me "Misraji your representation is likely to be accepted for one-month retention instead of two."

Unfortunately, the next day I was informed that even one month's retention was also not granted. My farewell was arranged and I got relieved on 30th April 2016 from Meerut for Gandhi Dham.

The following morning, I reached the Zonal Office, Meerut on the invitation of my boss Dr D.P. Singh. I had tea with him and then left for IGI Airport, New Delhi to take a flight to Ahmedabad. I reached Ahmedabad by 6 PM and then reached the residence of Mahesh Bhai Sahab. As usual, the hospitality of Mahesh Bhai Sahab and Meena Didi was awesome.

I left for Gandhi Dham branch early in the morning by a taxi booked by Mahesh bhai Sahab and reached there by 10.30 AM. At noon, I visited certain places in search of a residence. I found a good one and paid an advance of Rs. 5000. I spent my night in a hotel and the next day I had to go back to Lucknow in connection with a CBI case which was investigated by me. I left the branch post lunch and reached Ahmedabad, stayed with Mahesh Bhai Sahab, and took a flight early next morning.

As Amma was serious, I had taken permission from the bank to go on leave for a few days. After attending court at Lucknow, I came back to Kanpur. On coming to Kanpur, I was informed that I had been transferred to Bombay Market Branch, Surat. I was surprised that just after two days' tenure at Gandhi Dham branch, I had been transferred to Surat and was asked to join there without getting relieved from Gandhi Dham branch.

I reached Meerut from Kanpur to have other sets of clothes as the first ones were lying at Gandhi Dham. At 1 AM on the night of 16th May, I left Meerut for IGI Airport, New Delhi to catch a flight to Surat which was scheduled at 5 AM. Pankaj, who was also there in Meerut, accompanied me to the airport to catch a flight for Nagpur. Fortunately, one of my colleagues in Meerut, Shri Sunil Bhargava was posted in another branch of Surat. Sunil gave me a call and asked me to stay with him till I found my residence. When I landed, I found Sunil was at the airport. I boarded his car and reached his home.

I had showers at Sunil's place and then got ready for the office, of course, after having relishing breakfast made by Bhabhi ji. Sunil took me in his car and dropped me at my branch as well as introduced me to everyone. The present incumbent of the branch, Shri B.S. Khati was in the Roorkee branch when I was in Dehradun.

From Monday till Friday, I kept on moving for recovery of sticky loans with branch officials and in the evening searching for a house. I wanted to get a flat on lease in the same society where Sunil had been staying. Sunil was helpful again and one flat owner of his apartment agreed to have a lease agreement with me. It was planned to see the flat on Saturday 21st May but a meeting was convened by ZO on Saturday so it was decided to see the flat on Sunday. On Saturday, I reached the Zonal office, Ahmedabad with Sri Bothraji, AGM of Sunil's branch by his official car.

While coming back after the meeting, we stopped at a big Dhaba in Vadodara for dinner. It was 9.30 PM. Botharaji ordered the food. The moment food had been served on our plates; I received a call from Reena from Meerut. She was crying on the phone and saying "अम्मा नहीं रही, हम लोगों को छोड़ कर चली गई" (Amma is no more. She has left us behind). Tears rolled down my eyes and my entire life from childhood till date flashed before me. I was the closest to Amma not because I was the youngest but also because Amma had lived the most her life with me, or I can say I lived all the time with her. I had never dreamt of a life without her. I was in dilemma how to reach Kanpur to have Amma's last Darshan (Glimpse). As the dinner served in plate had been lying, Bothraji not only consoled me but also asked me to have some food.

I called Anil and requested "I am coming tomorrow; please do not cremate Amma till I reach."

He said "As per the doctor's opinion Amma had been on high medication for almost last two months, any delay in cremation may spoil the body. So, cremation would be done at the earliest the next morning."

I told all this to Reena also over the phone. Puja, who was also there, while crying told me over the phone "Papa Dadi had lived all her entire life with us and now neither you, nor mummy, nor I nor Shivam would be able to see Dadi for the last time, how unfortunate."

I lamented that had the Bank acceded to my request of my retention, for one or two months, at Meerut, I would have been beside my mother before her cremation. It was simply too painful to think that my entire family was not able to see Amma for the last time. I cursed and have still been cursing my luck.

Then Bothraji advised me to reach Mumbai and take a flight for New Delhi and therefrom reach Meerut. I called Shivam, told him about Dadi's demise and asked him to book two air tickets for New Delhi. I along with Bothara ji reached Surat which was almost between Ahmedabad and Mumbai. Out and out a gentleman Bothra ji forked out about Rs. 5 K and gave it to the driver and asked him to get the tank refilled and drop me in Mumbai. I took a couple of clothes. Sunil accompanied me up to Mumbai. We reached Mumbai at about 6 AM and the flight was a bit delayed. Sunil went back. Soon, thereafter, Shivam had come. We boarded the plane and reached New Delhi.

Pankaj was also informed about Amma's death. He took a flight from Nagpur to New Delhi which was about to reach soon after our flight.

We waited for Pankaj and then we three came to Meerut by taxi by noon. As the cremation had already been done, we reached Kanpur next day i.e., on 23rd May.

Now going down memory lane, I realize how cruel life had been with Amma. She lived with her husband, that is, our Pitaji for less than 25 years and without him for almost 43 long years. Even out of the 25 years with Pitaji, just 7 years were of quality married life. Such long years of widowed life could have broken any lady, but our Amma had kept her nerves all through and proved she was an iron lady. Mere thought of her turning a widow at an early age of 39 with additional responsibility of bringing up three kids, all under their teens, brings goosebumps to me. But Amma not only braved the roughness of life head-on but also sowed seeds of endurance in us. We could learn from her that Death is an event and grieving is a process. Only patience, self-belief and of course belief in God can take us through the upheavals of life. It was her sacrifice in life for us which made her an Ideal Mother and I am proud that she gave birth to me.

However, I recollect whenever she would get frustrated for any reason, she would say remembering Pitaji "तुम खुद तो चले गए हमे छोड़ गए." (You yourself have gone but left me behind).

Amma was Endurance personified, Patience personified, Perseverance personified, and an Ideal Mother personified. May her pious soul rest in eternal peace. Tathastu (Amen)...

...THE CLOSE SHAVE

Consequent upon my transfer from Meerut to Surat, I had been going by my car with Reena, Puja and little Bunny who was just two and a half months old. I had hired a driver. My household goods were sent by Agarwal Packers & Movers on 3rd June. We started in the morning of the 4th and after a brief stopover at Jaipur, where Puja had to do some shopping with Reena, we moved ahead and took lunch at a Dhaba on the highway and stayed at a hotel in Udaipur overnight. I asked the driver to have dinner and take a good sleep as we had planned to leave by 8 AM, the next morning.

After breakfast, we left the hotel and visited some lakes as desired by Puja. We took some photos and moved on. We passed through the city roads and reached the highway enjoying the scenic beauty and planning to come and enjoy the entire Rajasthan by taxi with Reena. I should mention that Reena was too fond of visiting places. In the meantime, perhaps I fell into a nap and when I woke up, I found myself on a stretcher at a hospital. I was told that our car had met with a serious accident at Rishabh Dev, a place which was an hour's drive away from Udaipur. I was also informed that my grandson was ok and Puja had fractured her wrist and gone to some relatives of Sheebu who fortunately lived in Udaipur. Reena was also injured and admitted in the same hospital, but she was not visible to me. The next day in the afternoon Anil, Bhabhi, Gita and Jijaji had also come from Kanpur and now we had our family members to take care of us, besides the staff of my Allahabad Bank and Punjab National Bank.

I was worried about Reena and wanted to assure myself that she was around and nothing adverse had taken place with her. I asked my Bhabhi "How is Reena and where is she?

"She is fine and lying on a bed at the other end of the ICU." Bhabhi replied

But I wanted to see Reena in person and asked Bhabhi to take me to her.

Bhabhi, somehow, could take me to the bed Reena was lying on. I took a sigh of relief. The next day Pankaj and Guddoo also came to the hospital from Hingan ghat and Lucknow respectively. Anil wanted us to be airlifted but the doctor did not permit him unless and until we had stabilised.

Later, I was advised that our car had hit the vehicle going ahead from my side which had led me to lose consciousness instantly. I also had started bleeding profusely.

Puja who had also been hit hard but remained in her senses. She later told me that she shouted "Papa.... Papa." She continued "Papa at that time, though I was in tremendous pain and worried about my little son, your situation led me to believe that something otherwise has happened with you. Moreover, you did not respond to my calls." As one of my bank branches was close by, its manager had rushed to the accident site. He could find my official visiting card in my pocket. He then sent a WhatsApp message on the official Bank group mentioning my extremely critical position. Most of the people later told me that they had thought, after going through the message, that I had died.

In the meantime, our goods had reached Surat and my friend Sri Sunil again came to our rescue. He managed to take the keys of the flat, which I was supposed to take on lease, from the owner.

The landlord, who had not seen me till then, was so generous that after knowing about my accident, allowed my goods to be stored in his flat without any lease agreement.

After getting stabilised, on 10th we started back from Udaipur to Lucknow by ambulance. Guddoo accompanied us in the ambulance. Puja had already left for Patna with Pankaj and Bunny by air. Puja later told me "Though Bunny, by God's grace and blessings, remained unscathed, he kept on crying for a couple of days." We all had a close shave but were safe. Thank you, the Almighty God.

We arrived in Lucknow and immediately went for Reena's MRI, which revealed she had two fractures in her spine. We were then transferred to a hospital and kept in the same room. We had some dreadful days in the hospital. Occasional movement of dead bodies kept me and Reena depressed but being together we could support each other. I had extreme difficulty in getting up from the bed because of severe pain in my chest and ribs. Reena was confined to the bed. We went to Reena's house after ten days in the hospital.

While I was in ICU in Udaipur, it was advised to me that one Mr. Jain, an industrialist, who had his marble factory just opposite to my accident site, was entering his factory at the time of the accident. He heard the skidding sound of car tyres and by the time he could have understood he saw a Wine Red car smashing into a truck loaded with cars. He rushed with his employees to offer help, immediately arranged two ambulances, and sent us to the hospital; besides he took, in his custody, all the goods being carried by us in our car under the impression that the goods, if left in the car, would get stolen. The very next day he came to the hospital and handed over the goods to my Jijaji.

After knowing his generosity, I called him one month later by arranging his mobile number and thanked him "Jain sir, it is me Arun Misra

"Arun Misra! Sorry I could not recognise you, sir." He responded.

"I am the same person whose life you saved while my family met with a very serious car accident near Rishab Dev. But for you, I would not have been here to talk to you. I and my entire family thank you from the core of our hearts."

"Oh, Mr. Misra. I see. Misraji it was only God who saved you and your family, not me." He spoke with all humility.

"Right sir, but had you not taken the initiative at the right time then you know what could have happened. I know God has saved us but that day you came as God for us." I thanked him.

"I am sure you; your wife and kids would be better now. Take care." He said and put down the phone.

In the meantime, Anil who was DGM & Head of Lucknow Circle of PNB made a request for my transfer back to Kanpur to our bank's FGM. A representation was sent on my behalf. My elder brother cum friend Shri P.K. Dixit, who held some senior position at the Trade union level also pushed my case hard and ultimately, I was temporarily transferred to Lucknow FGM span for three months. I requested Zonal Head Kanpur Shri A.K. Mahapatra sir to ask FGM sir to get me to his zone. Mahapatra sir advised that he had already done it and asked me to report at ZO, Kanpur on 4th July. As I was advised rest till 17th July by the doctor, I sought for permission to join on 18th and Mahapatra sir happily permitted the same.

I arrived in Kanpur on July 17th, reported for duty at the Kanpur zonal office the next day, and stayed at Anil's. I would go to Lucknow on a weekly basis as Reena was still recovering there from her spine fracture. Meanwhile, Reena's father died on July 22nd. It was another setback for us. In my absence, Reena's papa was taking care of Reena. He was a true gentleman who was always there for me. His death affected not just his family but also mine. May his soul rest in eternal peace. Amen... Later, on September 5th, I brought Reena to Kanpur.

Our joint stay at Anil's had started here from. After staying for a couple of months we moved to Gita's and then back to Anil's and this nomadic life continued for months. As I had been temporarily transferred for three months, I sent a request for an extension, and it was allowed. This temporary extension continued till January 2017.

As our luggage had reached Surat, we were here in Kanpur without anything, even had only a few clothes. We continued living that way. Reena was fed up with this style and would often say "I feel as if I have no existence of mine. I seem to be losing my confidence and feel low in my eyes."

"I understand but our goods are in Surat and we have nothing here with us. Bear with me for some more time. Things will change" I replied.

"Ask your bank either to get you transferred permanently to Kanpur so that goods are brought back or send you back to Surat where our goods are. I feel suffocated here." She continued "If you are not transferred permanently and kept here on a temporary basis, take a single room set here on rent. I promise, I will manage with bare minimum requirements. But for God's sake take me out from this life of piggy riding on others."

"Ok, I will see and talk to my boss." I consoled her.

I could understand the feelings of Reena. She had to live a life where she had no say. Moreover, Reena had always been a hard worker taking decisions on her own. She had been a homemaker of an independent house, so her feeling low and frustrated was not abnormal. Though I too felt a bit that way, and as the large part of my day would pass in the office, I did not feel that much frustration.

The only consolation had been that both of us were together and remained each other's strength. Our combined presence had been enough to sail us through these low times. Moreover, I always believed that this dark tunnel would end one day either because of my permanent retention at Kanpur or by going back to Surat again.

It bears mention that neither Reena nor I was ever denied any sort of right there at Anil's. It was a comfortable stay. We had been taken care of nicely, however the feelings we were having were normal as well.

In the meantime, Mahapatra sir got transferred and Ashok Patnaik sir had taken over the charge of the Kanpur zone. My hopes of any further support for my transfer to Kanpur got a massive blow. However, Patnaik sir turned out to be the biggest game changer for me.

This period of dependency upon others had continued till the 3rd of June when our Goods were brought back from Surat to Kanpur on the assurance of Patnaik sir. We took a flat on rent in Gulmohar Residency, Kalyanpur, Kanpur on the Bank lease. It had been a sheer coincidence that our Household goods were dispatched from Meerut for Surat on 3rd June 2016 and exactly after one year they were uploaded in my new rented flat on 3rd June, 2017. Reena had a sigh of relief as she was now going to live her independent life with me. It had been a moment of much awaited relief for both of us after that near death experience in 2016.

It is pertinent to mention here that Sunil had come to our help again as I did not have to go to Surat to bring my goods back to Kanpur. He managed all things and dispatched the already packed goods stored in Surat for Kanpur.

Good people like Jain sir, Sunil, Mahapatra sir and Patnaik sir are rare and difficult to find.

......LAUT KE NAHI AAUNGEE

Life is unpredictable. We never know what life has in store for us, and how it will unfold itself in the very next moment. Our knowledge in this regard notwithstanding, human beings keep planning for the days, months, and years together. I also had the same human weakness and was looking forward to my retirement due on 30th June, 2021, counting down my days and planning how to enjoy post-retirement life with Reena and the kids. But life had been hell-bent to prove itself highly unpredictable. In early January 2020, the COVID-19 virus had been traced in China's Wuhan City and gradually, the virus had started spreading across the world. No country in the world remained unaffected. By late February, it had made inroads into India as well. To curb the breakneck speed of the spread of the virus, the Prime Minister urged the nation to observe Janta Curfew on 22nd March. It was followed by the imposition of a Lockdown all over the country w.e.f. 25th March for 21 days, later extended up to 31st May. All modes of communication viz Railways, Airlines, Road Transport etc. had been put on a grinding halt. All offices and merchant establishments, barring sectors like Health, Police, Administration, Banking, and essential item shops, had been closed. The economy had started getting shattered and tens of thousands were sitting on the verge of losing jobs. Luckier ones got the opportunity to work from home (WFH).

However, Lockdown with relaxation continued for months together. Ours had been the toughest lockdown in the world. In view of the omnipresence of the virus across the world, it had been declared a Pandemic by WHO. The people were advised to wash their hands frequently, wear masks and keep a social distance of a minimum of six feet. I had always maintained that it should have been coined as Physical distancing, not social distancing as social distancing meant social disconnect whereas physical distancing meant physical disconnect. And, it was the physical disconnect that was the need of the hour. The people who tested positive were kept in quarantine for 14 days strictly in Hospitals. If a single COVID-19 patient was detected in a locality, the one-kilometre radius of the area was declared as a containment zone. We had pasted "Banking-Essential Services" stickers on the front and back windscreens of our cars for our smooth movement without being questioned by authorities. Though the fear and panic were too much, there was not much loss of human lives. By the end of 2020, the impact of Covid 19 had started receding and people almost started taking it as the normal flu.

Again, in the month of February 2021, COVID-19 had resurfaced with its new Delta Variant which by March end had taken the shape of a catastrophe. The spread of the virus had been so fast that enhanced medical facilities created during the first wave proved inadequate. There surfaced a huge shortage of logistics, be it Beds, medicines, Oxygen, and hospitals. Besides the genuine shortage of medicines. Some unscrupulous medicos had created artificial shortages to get inflated prices from needy persons. The media coverage had been absolutely frightening, full of horrible scenes of relatives of patients running from one hospital to another but not getting admissions. A scene was so pathetic where a wife, who could not get her husband gasping for oxygen admitted to a hospital, was seen giving mouth-to-mouth resuscitation to save her husband but unfortunately could not save him. The people at large had started avoiding watching such news as it was simply too depressing. As most of the hospitals were short of oxygen supply, the government had specially arranged Oxygen express trains for the transport of oxygen from manufacturing sites to different cities. Oxygen manufacturing plants were imported as well. A large swathe of people was seen lying outside the hospital buildings. The situation had turned so fearful that news of COVID-19 patients turning negative was almost rare.

As the situation got worse, the allotment of hospitals for admission, even in private ones, was taken over by the district administration. It would not be an exaggeration to say that Doctors themselves were unaware of proper treatment and it was just a matter of hit and trial. Besides, the doctors were reluctant to go close to the patients. Though social distancing was warranted to help prevent further spread of the virus, the distance maintained by the near and dear ones even from the attendants of the patients was turning too depressive and morale suppressing for attendants as well as patients.

It had started seeming that this disease would not diminish and it was going to be the end of the world. It looked like anyone who had tested positive would not survive. However, the government, this time, did not impose a Lockdown keeping in view the lesson it had learned from the adverse effect of the lockdown, imposed during the first wave, on the economy.

On 3rd April, my Mami, whom I always regarded as my second mother, expired. It was the third severest blow for me after the death of my Pitaji and Amma. I felt as if I had turned orphaned once again. Mami had supported and guided as well as financially helped us after Pitaji's demise. Even till her last breath mere visiting her had always boosted our morale. May her soul rest in peace and she continue to bless us from heaven. Amen....

Since early April 2021, Reena had started coughing. As Reena would get infected with cough and cold every year during March and April, so both of us took it as a once-a-year affair. Though COVID 19 had been happening all over the world, I did not take her cough that way. However, a couple of days after I thought it better to get Reena tested along with me. After the test, she was found positive on 20th April in the Rapid Test and RT-PCR also tested her positive later, however I tested negative. I immediately started her medication as while coming back home from the office, I had brought medicines fearing she might be found positive. An online consultation was also had with a doctor through one of my office colleagues Shruti Pawagi.

The same night I got a call from Shruti, daughter of my closest friend Hemant telling me "Chacha Papa has tested covid positive and he is getting worse every day but unwilling to get admitted to a hospital despite doctor's advice."

"Your Chachi too has tested positive. Anyways, get Hemant online." I told Shruti.

"He is sleeping," Shruti informed.

"Ok, ask him to call me tomorrow morning. By the way, what is the status of his Oxygen level." I spoke to her.

"It ranges from 90 to 93." She replied.

The next morning, I received a call from Hemant "Hi, my friend, my brother."

"Listen, you have beaten so many of our classmates during our college days. Now it is time to beat COIDV 19. I am sure you will do it. But please do get admitted to hospital." I advised him.

"Ok, but I have been having hiccups since morning. Anyways, talk to you later." He spoke to me and disconnected the phone.

On the 21st Reena's HRCT scan was done and her CT score was 7 out of 25. Technically and medically, it fell under the Mild category and there was nothing to worry about. Her Oxygen level was also well within a safe range.

It was about 5 AM on the morning of 22nd, I received a call on my mobile. It was a wailing Shruti on the other side saying "Chacha we are going to Hospital as Papa's oxygen level has dropped to 62 only. Please send some help, if you can."

I was shocked to hear this and could not find words to say anything. I wondered whom to send to help Shruti. I too was taking care of Reena all alone and such was the time as nobody was coming up for help, not even close ones.

While thinking about Hemant, Reena's Oxygen level also suddenly dropped to 87 and I got extremely frightened. I asked Reena "Please lie down in the prone position." Though Reena had difficulty in lying in a prone position because of her earlier Spine fractures, she did it and it improved her oxygen level a bit. In the interim, I talked to Jijaji and informed him about Reena's position. He managed to get a letter from CMO for Reena's admission to Krishna Super Specialty hospital. Now, I was in a dilemma about whether to admit Reena or not as there were more casualties among those who had been admitted to the Hospitals.

In the meantime, I received a call from profusely crying Shruti "Chacha Papa has gone. He has left us."

The news of Hemant passing away had got me shattered and broken. Tears rolled down my eyes as my best friend had gone. Hemant expired within five hours of leaving the home for the hospital and before he could get proper treatment. The hospital staff dealt with him casually while getting him admitted, which resulted in delayed start of treatment and ultimately to his tragic death. Hemant's going away had created a vacuum in my life. I had lost a friend cum brother. May his soul rest in peace. Amen…

But I had to hide it from Reena lest she got frightened. Hemant's death made me get Reena admitted to the hospital allotted to her without further delay.

I said to Reena "Let me get you admitted to the hospital for better treatment and care."

"Why? My position is stable." She spoke.

"Yes, you are stable. But on the safer side and medical care, it is better to go to the hospital." I replied.

" No, I will not go. Get me treated at home only." She spoke in a requesting tone.

"Reena, you know what has been happening around in the country recently. There is an extreme shortage of oxygen. Hospital beds are also not available. There is complete chaos and mayhem across the country. We are lucky that we have been allotted a hospital." I insisted.

"But, please do not take me to the hospital. I will be ok here at home soon." She pleaded.

"Please try to understand. If you do not get admitted and later the position gets worse, then what would be done? This hospital allotment will also go from our hands. So please….." I had put my point.

Reena looked at me silently and agreed to my persuasion, albeit unwillingly. With tears in her eyes, she said: "देखो चल तो रहीं हूं पर लौट के नही आऊंगी" (Ok, I would go but will not come back).

"Oh my God!" I was shocked to hear this.

Reena's statement sketched a dead body of Hemant before my eyes. I was trembling and fearing some untoward happening with Reena.

"Please do not say that. You will certainly come back home hale and hearty. Rather you will enter the home first while coming back from the hospital followed by me as you entered first during our home warming ceremony." I said with some unknown fear in my heart.

A silently sobbing Reena started keeping some clothes and necessities in a bag.

I took her to Hospital in my car. The concern for me had made her sit in the rear seat lest I got infected. One of my officers, Rajesh Sharma, husband of Shruti Pawagi, also accompanied me, of course in his car. After initial formalities, she was admitted to a private room. Anil and Bhabhi also reached the hospital. But they kept a distance which was keeping in view the social distancing guidelines.

When Reena was going to the allotted room, both of us looked deep into each other's eyes and waved hands to each other. It was an emotional moment as Reena and I were aware that we would now meet only when she was discharged from the hospital and that might take a minimum period of quarantine.

I took a seat at the entrance of the hospital near the reception and continued sitting there without eating proper food. I would manage with some patties or samosas. No doubt I was taking a risk of exposure to Covid-19. Everyone was asking me to avoid sitting in the hospital lest I caught the infection. But I had to be there as Reena was not only my wife, she was my life and mother of my kids as well. Each day I would come early in the morning and go back late in the evening. Reena had her phone with her, and I would keep talking to her at intervals. Video calls were also made.

On the evening of the 23rd. I managed to enter her room. She was lying in the bed and was surprised to see me. She said, "How did you get here?" It was prohibited to enter the room vis a vis the infectious nature of the disease. Reena then asked me "Go back lest you got infected. Anyways, bring some books and clothes for the next day." Despite Reena asking me to go back, her countenance loudly spoke that she was happy to see me.

At night, however, she complained about the indifferent attitude and casual approach of the medical staff. She also complained about the food. I took up the matter with doctors but things did not improve much.

Both Puja and Shivam had started putting pressure on me to let them come to Kanpur but I always denied lest they might get infected. On the afternoon of the 24th, I again sneaked into her room with the help of hospital staff. She asked me not to take unnecessary risks. She had been having a severe headache. Doctors gave her medicines, and when she felt better, I left for home.

JALDI AA JAO...JALDI AA JAO...

On the 25th morning, I was getting ready for the hospital after shower. I was planning to have a cup of tea before leaving home as my mother would often say that leaving home on an empty stomach might end up in no food during the rest of the day. At about 7 AM I received a call from Reena. On my picking up the call, came over her feeble and trembling voice, "जल्दी आ जाओ.... जल्दी आ जाओ..... जल्दी आ जाओ...." (come soon.... Come soon... come soon)

A shocked me asked " क्या हुआ.... क्या हुआ...." (What happened... what happened)

She simply repeated in broken voice: .... जल्दी आ जाओ....जल्दी आ जाओ."

I could comprehend that there was something serious with Reena and immediately called the hospital "Please see, the patient in the room seems to be under emergency."

"Let's see." Hospital staff said.

I dropped the plan of tea and refreshments and rushed towards the hospital thinking why an otherwise strong Reena had to speak in such a feeble voice expressing sheer helplessness. While I was in the lift of my society building, I received a call from the hospital "We have shifted her to ICU."

"Ok, you are a doctor, you must have taken the right steps. I am coming." I spoke and drove my car perhaps the fasted ever in my life. On reaching the hospital, I rushed to the ICU and found her on bed number 10 with an oxygen mask on. Her bed was the first from the entrance of the ICU. She looked at me with a sense of extreme helplessness. Though I was not able to ease her restlessness, I gestured to boost her morale.

The hospital staff asked me to take her belongings from the room she had been in for the last three days and handed over her mobile telephone to me. Mobile phones were not allowed in the ICU. The return of Reena's mobile to me meant the breaking of the only communication link between me and her.

Her shifting to ICU had made me panicky and lose my courage. I called Shivam "Beta Mummy has been shifted to ICU so now I ask you to come to Kanpur as psychologically and emotionally I feel very low and I need your support." Shivam said, "I have already been insisting to come over but you have not permitted me. Ok, do not worry I will be in Kanpur by the evening." He booked his air ticket via Lucknow.

In the meantime, the requirement for Remdesivir injection was thought of and Shivam arranged from Lucknow over phone from Mumbai. Poonam, Guddoo's wife booked a taxi and left for Kanpur with injections.

In the interim, an unusual incident took place. One nurse who had been sympathetic towards me for the last three days came to me at about 2 PM and asked me "Are you alone uncle?"

"Yes, however, my son is coming tonight. But why are you asking this? Is anything wrong with Aunty?" I inquired.

The nurse did not respond. I asked again but she kept mum and moved away with tears in her eyes.

As I was already perturbed, such a gesture of the nurse made me more panicky, and I thought Reena had expired. I called Shivam and told him "Beta mummy has gone."

"Oh no." Shivam cried over the phone and then thinking I was alone gathered himself and tried to boost my morale and said "Papa, hold your nerves. I am coming."

Puja was also informed followed by Anil and Gita. Puja was shocked and cried uncontrollably. I had to console her. My office mates too were informed. On hearing of Reena's demise, Apoorva Shivam's friend too got herself booked for Kanpur in the same flight with Shivam.

Anil, Gita Bhabhi, Jijaji, and Neeshu, my nephew all had come to the hospital in less than an hour. Poonam had also come with Remdesivir injections.

Jijaji Asked me "where did you get the news of Reena's demise from?"

I told him the whole story.

He wondered and asked me "Have you got it confirmed from anyone?

I said "No."

"You must have enquired and verified this." And then he went to the inquiry counter and enquired about the veracity of this news and it was found not correct.

Everyone had a huge sigh of relief. I thought that extremity of tension had made me such an idiot as I did not think it proper to get confirmation of this vital nature at my end and simply inferred based on the tears of a nurse. Everybody was relieved and information was passed on to both Puja and Shivam. They were too happy to listen to the information.

Some superstitions say that the fake news about someone's death enhances his / her age. So, I thought that this fake news would enhance Reena's life and she would return safely from the hospital. I prayed to God to let this superstition come true.

Shivam and Apoorva came to Kanpur through Lucknow by taxi arranged by me for bringing some more Remdesivir injections from Lucknow. I ensured that the dose of injection was not misused and administered to Reena only so I took the help of a nurse known through Lata Bhabhi, wife of Issac bhai. It was simply shameful that there was news of misuse of Remdesivir injections by hospitals.

Thereafter Reena's position kept swinging from satisfactory to serious. One day it looked like she was on the way to recovery and on the next day her position would deteriorate dramatically. Despite improvement, if any, in Reena's condition, doctors never said she was out of danger. They always maintained that such is the disease as they could not say anything with surety. Reena continued to fight for her survival. The fear of Reena's words before leaving home for the hospital had been haunting me and making me afraid of losing her off and on.

On the 26th, Puja called me and started crying. She wanted to come, see her mom, and help me tide over the grim situation. Despite my resistance fearing Puja, Pankaj, and little Bunny might get infected as well, she insisted and pleaded "Papa please let me come. I want to see mummy."

Though I was not inclined to let her come, Apoorva requested "Dad, let Puja di come otherwise she might fall ill there brooding over what is happening here."

I found weight in Apoorva's words and allowed Puja to come. On getting my nod to come, she along with Pankaj and Bunny boarded the next morning flight from Hyderabad to Lucknow and came to Kanpur and reached the hospital. Puja was the first to meet Reena inside the ICU with a PPE kit on.

Surprisingly after meeting Puja, Reena's Oxygen level improved drastically. This made me feel that meeting kith and kin bolsters the morale of a patient. I suggested to the doctors that in case of such contagious diseases as the patient's attendants were not allowed to meet him/her, unlike in other diseases, this led to a situation where the patient felt lonely and in extreme cases unwanted by the family, leading to depression and reduced immunity which ultimately proved fatal. I even suggested that, henceforth, ICU should have glass walls with thick curtains so that at pre-fixed times curtains were raised and attendants and patients could, at least, see each other. Doctors appeared to have listened to my suggestion only for the sake of it.

The next day onwards, Reena's position remained sometimes stable and sometimes critical. Then three or four days after her position started deteriorating. My heart had started coming to my mouth anticipating some untoward happening. My efforts to boost my morale have started giving in.

It bears mentioning that whenever I would peep into the ICU, Reena, in eye contact with me, would shake her hands as if she was either asking me not to come to ICU or saying she would not come back home. Till date I could not crack this puzzle. It is an enigma for me yet as only Reena knew what her bizarre gestures signified.

As I continued to visit the Hospital, Puja started taking strong objections to it and always asked me to either not to go to the hospital or come early.

One day when I got late coming back from the Hospital, she sent me a message "Papa please come back immediately. I do not want to lose both my parents" It was an emotional message which was indicative of the fact that Puja had started getting feelings of some untoward happening with Reena.

In the meantime, we had purchased a good number of PPE kits and Shivam would go to meet Reena by putting them on. Reena once asked Shivam for ice cream and desired to be shifted to Regency hospital, the best in Kanpur. But the sad part was that all the hospitals were full.

A couple of days thereafter, Reena's position deteriorated and she was put on a BIPAP machine.

During the visit to the hospital and peeping inside the ICU, I could sometimes see Reena begging for drinking water but doctors always denied her. I knew the continuous flow of Oxygen had been creating a burning sensation in her throat. How miserable these scenes had been that Reena was being denied even water notwithstanding her begging for the same! Though this was in line with a medical practice, for me, it was simply killing and I silently cried in the heart of my heart and prayed to the Almighty God to be on her side.

In the meantime, Pankaj and Shivam thought of contacting a senior and better chest specialist. We met Dr Rajiv Kakkar, the best Pulmonologist in Kanpur. He advised us to get a fresh RT-PCR test of Reena done and if she was found negative, options for a better hospital might be explored.

On 3rd May, we told Doctor Mehrotra at the hospital to get Reena tested again for COVID-19. Two days later, I and Shivam asked the Doctor "How is the RT-PCR report Doctor?"

“RT-PCR report is not yet received.” Said the doctor.

The reply infuriated me “What! The report is not received even after 24 hours whereas the reports are being received in 24 hours and moreover, here the test has been done in your hospital itself.”

"I have told the staff in ICU and also written in the case history file of the patient.” The doctor defended himself meekly.

"You simply advised the staff in ICU to get RT-PCR done, but did not ensure it was done or not.” I continued “Does your duty demand that much only? Doctor, please note if anything happens to my wife, I will file a suit against the hospital making you the main accused of murdering my wife.”

The doctor was shocked and terrified. He looked at Shivam as if he was complaining against me.

“Doctor, Papa is too disturbed, and that is why he has uttered all this. He does not mean it.” And then Shivam asked me, “Papa just hold on and please wait outside the room.”

I came out of the doctor’s chamber but Shivam continued discussing with him.

Later, we went to the ICU and asked the doctor on duty if Reena had been tested or not for RT-PCR. To our utter surprise, we found Reena's test had already been done and the report reached the hospital in the morning itself before the doctor’s visit. It was COVID negative report. How irresponsible Doctor Mehrotra had been that he did not think of enquiring about the report and simply lied before us. Such doctors need to be booked and taken to task. They are bloody mercenaries and play with the lives of the patients.

As the report was favourable, we had a sigh of relief and started thinking Reena would be normal soon. We tried to get Reena into a better hospital in the city but failed. Through Reeshu we applied pressure from one State Cabinet Minister for getting admission to the Regency Hospital.

Under pressure from the minister, the doctor in Regency Hospital said "We can admit your patient in the ICU but the catch is that we do not have any surplus Ventilator. In case your patient suddenly requires a Ventilator, we may find ourselves handicapped."

We had nothing to say. I thought, perhaps, the hospital was trying to kill two birds with one stone. One, they could please the cabinet minister that they were ready to admit the patient but attendants were reluctant for want of the ventilator, two, they also kept us in good humour that we were not denied admission outrightly. We, therefore, had no option but to keep Reena at the mercy of those irresponsible doctors at Krishna hospital. Even the question of plasma transfusion had started popping up. We tried our best but matching plasma was not available. My earlier office colleague Mrinal got a request aired on one FM radio requesting listeners to arrange Plasma for B Negative blood group. The request was aired for a few days.

As luck would have it, on the 7th Reena's position deteriorated and we got a call from hospital "We have put your patient on Ventilator." I helplessly listened to this information and prayed to God to save Reena. I contacted my college friend Dr Ashutosh Tiwari, a nephrologist and settled in the USA. I asked him "Ashu, what are the chances of revival of a patient who has been put on a ventilator?"

"Arun, there are many instances where patients who remained on a ventilator for weeks together have bounced back and are living a normal life." Ashutosh, I thought, did not want me to lose hope.

I am a religious person but not as much as Reena but I had started reading Sundar Kand twice a day. Chanting of Maha Mritunjay Mantra was also started by me. After having gone on Ventilator, Reena's position had become such critical as shifting to another hospital had almost been ruled out. We had been hoping against hope. On the advice of doctors, we also arranged immunosuppressants and two doses were administered to Reena as well. We all had been living under the fear of the unknown which had started looking almost certain to happen. The anticipatory death had started taking a heavy toll on all of us.

LIFE HAD PAUSED ON ME

It was 1.30 AM on the night of 8th and 9th of May 2021. I was in the kitchen fetching a glass of water for myself and suddenly my mobile phone, lying in the bedroom, started ringing. I rushed to the bedroom only to find Puja had already picked up the call. My heart had almost missed a beat thinking it must be a call from the Hospital as no friend of mine was expected to call at this time. After the call, I could not muster courage to ask whose phone call it was. Puja on her own told me "Papa, It was a call from the hospital informing that mummy had a cardiac attack a short while ago, however, she could be revived through CPR."

It was a massive blow for us. I could guess that the bell had rung for Reena. I laid on the bed silently with an immense amount of fear in my heart. I had started chanting Maha Mritunjay Mantra and thought how unfortunate I was that my Reena, struggling for life, had suffered a cardiac attack and I could not meet her in the ICU because of COVID-19 restrictions. I kept on praying to God believing he would certainly save my Reena for me and my kids. Besides, I thought the puja already arranged by a pandit might work wonders. My kids kept sitting beside me holding my hands in theirs.

At about 4.30 AM, another call came from the hospital bringing my heart to my mouth. Puja picked up the call. Then Shivam took the phone from Puja. Their body language was speaking volumes that the God Almighty had decided to put me through the toughest times of my life. Before I could ask, both of my kids came close to me and said "Papa, mummy has gone."

My life had just paused on me, and my body got rooted to the spot. The walls caved in, and my world ended in a split second. I had turned numb and frozen. Suddenly my body started shivering which led to tremors. Both Puja and Shivam as well as Pankaj held me tightly. All three kids, despite being too sad themselves, kept a bold face before me.

Puja later told me while sobbing "Doctor said that mummy had a repeat cardiac attack but this time the CPR could not work and Mummy lost her battle for life."

I heard all this with eyes open.

It is rightly said that the hardest of times bring out the true mettle of a person. I really got some divine power giving me strength that got me through the unimaginable situation I was in. I asked Shivam "Beta enquire from the hospital when should we Reach the hospital to bring the body of Reena."

I thought about how cruel the world was. A little while ago, I was using the word "Reena" and now, the word "Body." This screwed me but this is what we address to a dead body. On contact by Shivam the hospital authorities advised to come after 9.30 AM to take Reena's body. All relatives were informed about Reena's sad demise.

Within two hours Anil, Bhabhi, Jijaji, Gita and others reached home. Later, Reeshu and Guddoo with their wives reached directly to the Hospital.

While waiting for the 9.30 to strike, I had plunged into a flashback. I wondered if it was a simple premonition about her death that Reena uttered those words before leaving for the hospital. I also thought about how committed Reena had been to her word. She had always honoured her word and never gone back on it. I started repenting that despite being aware of her penchant for keeping her word, I could not understand this and took her to the hospital for admission even after she had uttered that she would not come back if admitted to the hospital. I was cursing myself and finding myself guilty of killing her. Reena had kept her last word as well and left us with a void that could never ever be filled. The pain and agony might diminish but the scar would remain forever. Her last words before going to the hospital still reverberate in my ears...

"देखो चल तो रहीं हूं पर लौट के नही आऊंगी".

My life had gone, and my dreams had been shattered. Life had started looking like an endless tunnel with no light visible at the end. I was thinking Reena had left with several unfulfilled dreams like getting Shivam married and welcoming her Bahu (Son's wife) and babysitting for her Pota/Poti (Son's kids) besides traveling extensively with me post my superannuation. I, now, think had she been in senses before she breathed her last, how restless she would have been in finding neither me nor her kids before her whom she had lived all her life and sacrificed all her happiness for. I believe she must have cried loudly calling my and the kids' names in absolute helplessness and restlessness.

उसने न जाने कौन सी आह भरी होगी
जाते जाते उसने आवाज तो दी ही होगी

(I do not know how she would had sighed, I am sure
she would have cried for me before passing away)

Mere imagination of the pains she would have undergone in her last moments gives a shudder in my spine and makes me cry in utter pain and feel guilty why I was not beside her at that moment.

The scene of Reena begging for water had also been flashing before my eyes and I cried within me that my Reena has left the world even thirsty.

Reena's journey that kicked off on the 23rd of February 1963 had been a tumultuous one viz the complications during her first as well as second pregnancies, removal of her uterus 2001, spine fractures after the accident in 2016 and again in 2019 while she slipped in a Hotel in Agra and finally ended abruptly at the wee hours of 4 AM on the 9th of May 2021 after giving me two wonderful kids and lots of memories to cry for and smile on. May her pious soul rest in eternal peace and we meet again up above in heaven. Tathastu (Amen)....

……THE LAST JOURNEY

Shivam and Pankaj left for Hospital at 8.30 AM, and I was forced by my kids to stay back at home. I had planned to bring Reena's body in the premises of my society but Shivam called me from the hospital and advised "Papa I opine we should not bring mummy's body to the society's premises lest anyone should get infected in days to come. And, if this happens the onus would be fixed on you. People would say that Misraji's wife, who died of COVID, brought the infection into society. You know, no one knows Mummy had tested negative before passing away."

I agreed with Shivam. Really, he had come of age, I thought. I asked him "Yes, you are correct beta. You bring the body in an ambulance and keep it outside the society's building under the big Banyan tree where we all will pay homage to her and then proceed to the cremation site for the last rites."

Rena's body was brought in an ambulance. It was wrapped in a plastic cover, but her face was open and we could see it. It was very pathetic to see her lying lifeless in the ambulance. Her face looked as if she had died in pain. Some drops of blood had oozed out of her nostrils. I could not gaze at her for long. Both puja and Shivam came to me crying and held me tightly. I hugged them and promised in a shivering tone "Do not cry beta. Now I am your Mummy and Papa both and I will give love and care of both as well." And then we all broke down. Many people who had been passing by on the roads were seen having tears in their eyes after watching my kids crying on my shoulders.

All others including Pankaj, Gita, jijaji, Anil, Bhabhi, Reeshu and Guddoo, etc. were either crying or were deeply shocked.

Nearby walkers and society members were standing sad with teary eyes. Soon, we male members boarded the cars for Reena's last journey to Bhairon Ghat (Cremation site). While boarding the car, I could see Puja crying profoundly and while the ambulance started crawling, she was trying to see it as far as she could. I was just having my eyes welled, doing my best lest tears rolled down.

We had reached Bhairon Ghat for the last rites of Reena. Her body was in the ambulance and Reeshu accompanied her body. On reaching there, I found some of my office colleagues, Menon sir, Oshiher Chaudhary, Abhishek Gupta, Shekhar, Ankur, Darvesh, Abhishek Mishra, Vivek Mishra, Arpit Gupta, etc. were already present. There was a huge rush in the electric crematorium and tokens were being issued for cremation. It had been a telling story of the massacre being perpetrated by COVID -19.

First, Shivam reached the Electric crematorium thinking the body had to be cremated as per covid norms. But when authorities saw the Death Certificate having a mention that Reena had turned Corona negative prior to her death, it was advised to cremate her as per traditions. Reena's body was, therefore, brought to the ghat where cremation as per traditions had to be done.

Reeshu called me to come over for the final rites. Reena had expired as a Suhagan (husband being alive), all Shringar (decoration of a married lady) was done as per Hindu traditions. Reeshu asked me to see her for the last time, but watching my Reena dead with the full shringar of a suhagan was something beyond my courage. My heart was pumping blood like anything. Reena's body was given a wash and put on the pyre. I was asked to perform all the rituals which I did. Now the time had come for lighting the pyre. Five persons including me and Shivam roamed around the body five times and ultimately, I lit the pyre. I thought that I had not only lit the pyre of Reena's mundane body but the pyre of my love, my hopes, my ambitions, my dreams, and my entire existence.

The pyre of Reena had caught the fire in full bloom. Sitting at a distance from the burning fire, several questions popped up within me. I questioned myself about my love for Reena and thought about how I could light her body on fire whereas a small burn of her in the kitchen always made me uneasy and I would do anything to ease her pain. It was nothing but the dichotomy of life where a mandatory ritual occasionally looks unacceptable and develops assorted feelings of guilt and anger. I started cursing myself why I was simply watching her burn from a safe distance as a spectator and doing nothing to douse the fire and save Reena. Surrounded by millions of thoughts, I wondered if all this happens in life, then why all this happens and if life itself is so, then why life is so, and if life is so, then do we come here only to get separated, grieve, and bear the unbearable pain? There was no one to offer answers to these weird questions popping up within me. The thought process did not stop there. I had started comparing human beings with animals and thought how better the animals were than us as they did not have the brains to understand what life was all about. I thought I was paying the price for being a rational animal called a human. While I was lost in thoughts with tears flowing down, one of my officers, Abhishek Mishra hugged me tightly and tried to console me.

After an hour, we left Bhairon Ghat only to return the next morning to pick up PHOOLS (those portions of the skull which are not completely burnt) and flow them into the river Ganga.

I reached HOME and found that it had turned into a HOUSE, a structure of brick and mortar. Though all were present, the soul of the home, my Reena, was missing. The pyre was burning there at the ghat, and my heart was burning with anger and pain here in the house.

I sat on the sofa staring blankly. The wheel of time had started spinning backwards and nostalgia took me in its grip. I reminisced the day when I saw Reena for the first time, the day of our marriage and Jaimal when she almost fainted, her coming to my home for the first time, our honeymoon, her beaming and blushing face when she made me aware of her pregnancy, her traumatic phase during the pregnancy and before Puja's birth, her shining face on becoming a mother for the first time, her worried face when had come to know that the entire blood of her newly born baby, Puja, had to be changed, her crying face when she was informed that her second baby, still in her womb, might not be saved and then sheer happiness on Shivam's safe birth, her worried face during Shivam's sickness, her happiness on Puja's marriage with Pankaj and then becoming Nani after Bunny's birth, her supporting me during lows of my life and specially after the near-fatal car accident and thereafter while staying with me at multiple places like nomads and then happiness on owning a flat, her saying those shocking words before leaving for the hospital, her calling me from the hospital and saying in feeble voice to come soon, her waving hand from the ICU bed and her folded hands begging for water and requesting Shivam for ice cream and shifting to Regency hospital. I was also repenting that had I not let her sit on the rear seat of the car while taking her to the hospital, I would have got the one more opportunity of traveling together and sitting close to her. Besides, I recollected during our housewarming ceremony, Reena had entered the home before me but today I entered the home with Reena neither ahead of nor behind me. While I was having flashbacks, tears started rolling down drop by drop. Pankaj, Puja, and Shivam had come from behind and put comforting hands on my shoulders, hugged me and offered me a cup of tea. While sipping my tea, suddenly two lines came to mind…

"बहुत कुछ मर जाता है भीतर मेरे ये सोच कर
कि तुमसे जुदा हो जीना है अब मुझको जीवन भर"

(A lot of things just die within me, when
I think I must live sans you rest of my life)

As the evening started falling, all gradually left leaving only Puja, Pankaj, Shivam, Apoorva, and Little Bunny. The loneliness which was a few inches away in the presence of so many people started inching towards me, finding fewer people. Everyone was crying but hiding it from each other. I too wanted to cry loud but being the head of the family, I had no option but to control my emotions lest it might weaken the morale of my kids who were putting on false brave faces before me.

The next morning, I along with Shivam reached Bhairon Ghat to pick up the PHOOLS. We picked PHOOLS and let them flow with the sacred water of the river Ganga. I and Shivam kept our hands folded praying to God Almighty to let Reena have a place under his feet. We kept watching the bigger portion of PHOOLS sinking in the Ganga and lighter ones flowing down with the water. Our eyes were teary, but we had restrained ourselves keeping in view the saying that tears made the departed soul restless.

The last site of Rena's existence, her ashes, was just inching away from us forever and we were mere numb and shattered spectators.

At noon, Co-residents of the society viz Dixitji, Dr. Bhagoliwal, Jain sahab, Khattarji Varunji, Dr Mehrotra etc came calling to express their solidarity with me in this hour of crisis. Some of them said to reminisce about sweet moments shared with Reena and try to be happy but the fact was that remembering those moments sunk my heart. There were others who said I should not think of Reena and if any thought of her even crossed my mind, I better avoid it. But no one could tell me if any switch was available that could be installed in our bodies and kept in "Put On" or "Put Off" mode to check our emotions playing with us. There were some who picked up the philosophical route saying that whosoever had come would go as life was nothing but a stage where everyone's entry for playing the role and exit after the role was predetermined, hence I must not cry. Reena had that much association with me, some suggested and she had reached her ultimate home.

I knew what my neighbours were saying was correct and I too would have consoled anyone that way, but as a sufferer, such sermons instead of soothing were rather irritating me. It was "easier said than done" like situation and yet another example of life's dichotomy.

Final Day of Mourning

Reena's Tehranvi was scheduled on 21st May 2021. As Corona was still creating havoc, it was decided to keep it in a low profile, and with only a few close members of the family that included I, Puja, Pankaj, Bunny, Shivam, Anil, Bhabi, Jijaji, Gita, Guddo, Poonam, Reeshu, Raji, Mama, Mikki, Babloo, Yogesh, Kshma Di, Neeshu etc. Apoorva had gone back as her professional commitments were getting affected and she had been here for almost three weeks.

100 food packets were made and packed for distribution among needy and hungry persons.

Puja was done by a priest and I did all the rituals. It was a very emotional moment for me as almost two years back on 23rd February 2019, we had a puja in connection with our Home-warming when I and Reena sat side by side exactly at this point where today Reena's photo was kept on a pedestal and below that, a Diya (small earthen pot with oil and a wick) was lit. Puja was sitting beside me and could not prevent herself from sobbing. Shivam was putting on a brave but fake front. Pankaj and others looked sombre and sad.

After Puja, I went to distribute packaged foods to people sitting outside temples. I visited about 7 temples. I came back after distributing food and took one plate full of food to put under a tree.

The next day after Tehravi, Pankaj too left for Latur via Hyderabad. I along with Puja, Shivam and Bunny went to drop him off at Lucknow airport. Pankaj's departure reduced the number of persons at home to four and made us lonelier.

After a long gap of more than a month, I reported back to duty on 24th May. All my colleagues were very sympathetic towards me.

While coming back from the office on this day my eyes welled up remembering Reena who of late had started calling me in the evening, asking "किधर हो? ऑफिस से निकल लिए?" (Where are you? left the office?). I knew no such call would come henceforth.

Shivam was scheduled to leave for Mumbai on 27th because of his professional commitments. Now the question was if I would continue my stay in my flat with Puja and Bunny or leave for Anil's place as both Anil and Bhabhi had been insisting. I asked Puja if she would be comfortable staying in the flat with Bunny only till, I was out for the office. Though she did not utter anything, her body language suggested she was nervous about staying only with Bunny. I could comprehend and decided to move to Anil's place after Shivam's departure to Mumbai on 27th. Bhabhi wanted us to come early to her place so that Shivam might also stay with them for a few days.

After coming back home from the office on the 24th evening, I along with Puja, Shivam, and Bunny left for Anil's place.

On 27th, we left for Lucknow to drop Shivam at Lucknow airport for his onward journey to Mumbai. After Shivam's departure, I felt a huge vacuum and was unwilling to come back to Kanpur. I had been feeling highly depressed to reach Kanpur where Reena would not be around and Shivam, who had been with me for more than a month, had gone back to Mumbai after staying for the longest time with me since his leaving to Mumbai for his studies in 2011.

I unnecessarily drove along the roads of Lucknow with Puja and Bunny and even in Kanpur took a longer route to reach home. I could realize this was nothing more than escapism from reality. But a numb and highly disturbed mind was trying to find succour in this escapist route but in vain.

...THE DAY OF HANGING BOOTS

For more than the last one year, I had been eagerly awaiting the day of hanging my boots. I was looking forward to growing old together with Reena, roaming here and there. I had been rather counting down the days before I got retired. Every day, I would say that now only so many months and days were left. This counting down had become a regular process to such a level as one day I told my friends and colleagues that I was afraid if the Almighty God had also been counting my days and would pick me up for my final journey before my day of retirement and say "Forget about retirement from the bank, enjoy your final retirement buddy." This thing had been said in a lighter vein, just heard and smiled away by all. But later, I realized that God had genuinely been counting days, not for me but for my Reena and took her away from my life just one month and 22 days before the most awaited day of my superannuation i.e., 30th June 2021.

My Zonal Head, Menon sir who had applied for voluntary retirement was also getting retired on the same day. A party was organized by my colleagues at a hotel.

As per prevailing practice, the wives of retiring officials were also invited, so in absence of Reena, Puja was given an invite. She was brought to the hotel by one lady officer Ayushi Tewari. Puja sat on the first row, and I was on the dais along with Menon Sir and his wife, B.B.K. Vinai sir (unfortunately no more with us now) and incoming Zonal Head Bhatia sir.

While the function was going on, I saw Puja sobbing so I asked one lady officer, Shruti Pawagi to sit beside her.

And, when I was asked to deliver a speech, I was very sad and before I finished my speech, my eyes welled up, and all my efforts to rein in tears from flowing down failed. I could not complete my speech. My friends came close and comforted me.

Guddoo along with his daughter Khushi had also come. My earlier Zonal Head, Shri Patnaik sir had sent many gifts including one beautiful video of me, one photo frame with my photo and good words for me, an Alexa, a Suit length, and a shirt and tie. Office colleagues had given me a mobile phone and many other things.

At last, my colleague Abhishek Gupta dropped me at home as Puja had already gone home with Ayushi. Thus, the most awaited day of retiring from the bank went off on a sombre note, and all the excitement which I had been thinking for the last many months had died with Reena. It is true that man proposes, and God disposes.

Came, 1st July 2021 and it was the first day after superannuation. The plans to visit the kids for enjoyment had just gone in the air. Now it was a matter of my existence and survival. How to carry on and which thread to be picked up to create a new fabric of life were the big questions. The mere thought that life had to be passed off this way only having nothing in hand to do was enough to shake me. Initial days passed off in going to the office to see whether terminal dues were received or not. Coming back from the office always pinched me as Reena's absence was badly missed.

As I had never lived alone earlier, and hence, it was pretty sure that I was not going to stay in Kanpur all alone and had to move to either Anil's or Puja's or Shivam's place. The faintest of imaginations did not give me a chance of living alone and this made Puja stay back at Kanpur till superannuation and take me to her place. Post-retirement, I passed off 10 more days in Anil's place.

On 10th July 2021, I booked my personal car for Mumbai for Shivam's use through a transporter as there appeared no reason to keep the car in Kanpur when I was to stay with kids. I had booked Myself, Puja, and Bunny by air for Mumbai via Lucknow on 11th, I had received my Provident Fund, Gratuity, and Leave encashment. The same was invested as per my wisdom.

ILL AT EASE

I, Puja, and Bunny left Anil's on 11th morning for Lucknow airport to catch a flight for Mumbai. I saw tears in the eyes of both Anil and Bhabhi. Guddoo and Reeshu with kids had reached the airport to see us off. My old RBI friend Pankaj Srivastava too made it to the airport. I reached Mumbai in the late evening. Shivam and Apoorva had come to the airport to receive us. After reaching Shivam's flat, we refreshed ourselves and after dinner had some gossip and then retired for the day. The next day, Apoorva's mummy had come from Jaipur to discuss the marriage of Shivam and Apoorva. After the exchange of pleasantries, we discussed and agreed to the relationship but as told by Apoorva's mummy, marriage was unlikely to happen before November 2022 because of some stellar constellations. On 15th, we left Mumbai for Latur and reached there on the 16th morning.

The initial days at Latur passed off in a normal manner but almost after two weeks, the loss of Reena which was always hard on me had started hitting me harder. The feeling that I was not going to see Reena in my remaining life was disquieting. The pain of having left my flat whose interiors were tastefully decorated by Reena as well as parting from friends was very unsettling.

After a few days of stay in Latur I started missing Reena more because I had no acquaintances to pass time with except Puja, Pankaj, and Bunny. But Pankaj was awfully busy with his bank and would reach home not before 10 PM at night. His desire to share time with me notwithstanding, he did not have time. However, he would give me as much time as he could manage. It would not be an exaggeration if I say he did not have time even for himself. Puja being the daughter had limited disciplines to talk about with me, though she always pushed me to smile and mix with people in her society. The Little Bunny though gave me time but generally preferred to play with his little friends. Too much of surplus time with nothing to do had been often making me go down memory lane leading to missing Reena more.

In Latur I would sleep in the first-floor room all alone. Not only would I sleep late but also get sleep broken within two or three hours. Thereafter, I would keep tossing and turning in bed, anxiously waiting for the day to happen. I would leave the bed in the wee hours of the morning only to walk around in society for hours together despite having pains in my knees. After coming back from the walk in the morning, I would sit in the portico and stare blankly. As I would not get proper sleep at night, I would feel heavily sleepy in the day time but the saddest part was that some unknown fear always held me back from sleeping in the daytime. A mere drop of the eyelid and some fear would make my eyes wide open. Such was the helplessness that words fail me to describe. The feeling of having lost everything had enveloped me. Life had started looking meaningless and certainly not worth living. I had been dying a bit every moment.

The uneasiness had increased to such a level as I had no option but to start putting myself on antianxiety and sleeping pills. I started taking one antianxiety tablet at 4 PM and another one at 6 PM followed by a sleeping pill before retiring to bed. The situation was so grim that if there was any delay in popping the tablet, I would feel sinking. Once, I was out of the house and not keeping the anti-anxiety tablet with me. By 6.30 PM my position became such as I had to request the medical store to give me just one tablet but the salesman was reluctant to give me even a single tablet without the doctor's prescription. However, after looking at my gloomy face and considering my repeated requests, he agreed to give me just one tablet. I popped the tablet immediately and after half an hour only I was a shade better.

My precarious position had made Puja and Pankaj a bit worried about me. One day Puja asked me "Papa, of late, I and Pankaj have been observing that you are uncomfortable here and keep staring blankly. If you do not feel comfortable here, you are free to take your call to stay anywhere, either with us or Shivam or with Bade Papa (Anil) in Kanpur."

"Nothing like that," I replied evasively but the fact was that staying with kids meant continuing the life with my recognition just as the father of Puja and Shivam, father-in-law of Pankaj and grandfather of little Bunny. Nobody knew I was Arun. Carrying on in life with secondary and tertiary identities looked meaningless. Simultaneously, mere thinking of coming back to Kanpur would scare me in dreams as well. I was in a fix.

Here only I could realize that Life was listless without friends as they are the elixir of life and provide a vent to our feelings. Sans friends passing time only with Shivam, Puja, Pankaj and Bunny had started looking difficult. Though Puja, Pankaj and Shivam took the best care of me, I had failed to find relief. They took me to markets, Temples, and other places as well. I had also started going to the temple of Puja's society in the morning and evening for puja and chanting bhajans.

To find peace, I visited Karnataka to Sheebu's place, my elder niece, with Puja, Pankaj, and Bunny. After staying there for three days, I was back again at Latur. The peace was still elusive, though these three days passed off peacefully.

In the meantime, my ex-boss Patnaik sir and his wife, Soma Bhabhi counselled over phone "Misraji your mind is unstable and the situation is too fluid as of now. You just carry on in life by visiting here and there and taking a call after some time."

Patnaik sir had also advised, "You need some time and space before you could concentrate logically and take a pragmatic call. But note that your own flat would provide you the peace of mind you have been exploring here and there, even if it calls for staying alone."

He continued "I know, it would be challenging to start with but believe me if you could hold your nerves and bear the initial jerks, it would make you stronger and life worth living. Staying with others would simply make you live a life without independence. Remember the quote...tough times do not last, tough people do."

The idea of Patnaik sir was suggestive of the fact that we could not always control things and are often required to flow with time, have deep faith in self and the God Almighty and let go of the past. He also invited me to visit him in Chandigarh.

Though the idea of Patnaik sir was practical, it appeared too intimidating to me. However, it also ignited a faint idea simmering within me "Can I live in my flat all by myself...Should I take one chance to test myself?"

My heart had started looking committed to finding a solution vis a vis challenges thrown by life instead of opting for an escapist route.

During this period of turbulence, I received a call from the zonal office that a summon from the CBI court had been received at their end asking me to report at CBI Court, Lucknow on 6th August as CBI witness in a case which had been investigated by me. The Zonal Office mailed the summon to me. I reached Lucknow on the 5th. On the scheduled date, the court was closed on account of the lawyer's strike. The next date was fixed for the 23rd of August. As there was enough time gap, I found this was an opportunity to visit Kanpur. I also decided to visit New Delhi where Gita was at Shilpi's place with Jija ji. I also thought of visiting Patnaik sir. I booked tickets for traveling to New Delhi on the 12th, then onwards to Chandigarh on 16th thinking I would get some peace of mind meeting Gita, Patnaik sir etc.

In SEARCH OF PEACE

As per plan, I reached Kanpur on the 8th. On the 9th I visited the Zonal Office Kanpur where one of my colleagues, Sanjay, advised that applications for the empanelment of concurrent auditors in the Bank had been invited. Sanjay advised me to apply for it, as it would not only keep me engaged but give a reason and support to stay at Kanpur also, if only I wanted. There was no denying that staying with kids or Anil as also getting due respect and care from them had not provided me that much relief I had been searching for. Staying at Kanpur all alone was the only option left that was not explored yet. Sanjay's advice looked quite convincing and after initial reluctance, I agreed to apply. Sanjay had prevailed upon me and my application was submitted online on the same day. The faint idea of staying at Kanpur, ignited by Patnaik sir, had started taking shape.

On 12th August, as per the prefixed program, I proceeded to Delhi and reached Shilpi's place. I visited a few places including Gurugram with Parth, Shilpi's husband. Shilpi was on the family way those days. I had some temporary relief there at Shilpi's. After staying there for four days, I left for Chandigarh on the 16th morning to stay with Patnaik sir. My ex-colleague of Kanpur Rajnish Chaudhary, posted at Chandigarh, had come to receive me at the Station. I was nicely welcomed by Soma Bhabhi. Patnaik sir who had gone to Chennai had also come about an hour after my arrival. I enjoyed the evening in the Chandigarh club with Patnaik sir, the next day in Himachal Pradesh and a day thereafter in Amritsar with Rajnish Chaudhary. I visited the Golden Temple and prayed to the Almighty to provide peace of mind so that I could live peacefully.

On the 21st, I returned to Delhi with Patnaik sir, Bhabhi and the kids by a taxi and reached back to Shilpi's place to celebrate Raksha Bandhan on the 22nd. I took the Tejas train to Lucknow on the same day to attend the CBI court case on 23rd.The peace had still been elusive but these few days did provide me temporary relief.

The train had a stopover of 5 minutes at Kanpur but as the train had come before the time it stayed put for 25 minutes. Unusual feelings had just enveloped me. I thought had Reena been around I would have booked my tickets for Kanpur and dropped here, only to leave for Lucknow the next day. But as she was no more, I had booked for Lucknow straight. I felt restless as it was for the first time when I was passing through Kanpur and not getting down. At the actual departure time, the train started and reached Lucknow.

Because of the death of the ex-CM of UP, Kalyan Singh, it was declared a holiday in court on 23rd, and the next date was fixed for the 7th of September. Finding ample time between two dates, I went back to Kanpur again on 25th

Some of my closest colleagues of the Zonal Office had planned a small dining out at Cawnpore Club on the 25th evening. Shekhar, Abhishek, Ankur, and I reached the Cawnpore club and enjoyed our food and had some gala time there. All of them collectively gifted me a beautiful smart watch. Such get-togethers post-Reena's demise had always been soothing at least for that short period. Abhishek, later, dropped me at Anil's place and went off. Sumi, Bhabhi's maid, opened the door and after a brief chat with Anil and Bhabhi, I went upstairs to my room and retired for the day.

I jumped on the bed and fell asleep but my sleep got broken within half an hour. It was quite unusual to get my sleep broken at such a short interval after sleeping. I applied all trusted tricks for inducing sleep but failed. Not only my efforts to fall asleep had been falling apart but simultaneously a sense of intense uneasiness started enveloping me. Restlessness had reached such a level as I could not close my eyes for it made me feel sinking into the deep sea. Unusual thoughts had started hitting from all around. I got up and started walking in the room. And, when I found all my efforts were of no use and uneasiness getting unbearable, I wished to go out on the terrace to have fresh air and a view of the road down below. The moment I opened the door, the pitch darkness and eerie silence outside just frightened me. I immediately banged the door closed. The fear of the unknown had just taken me in its grip. I jumped on the bed only to get up again with tears rolling down from my eyes. I looked upward and cried "Hey God! What this is all about. You have snatched my Reena and now snatched my sleep and peace as well." I further pleaded "Either let me live a normal life or take me up to Reena." But there had been no one around to listen to my yearnings.

I was strolling in the room again, slapping my face and stretching my hair and crying. The entire night passed in my eyes and I looked at my watch, it was around 3.30 AM. To get rid of this vicious cycle and divert my mind, I started sending messages to some of my friends who later asked me in the morning why I was awake so early.

Thus, the entire night passed off in such a frightening atmosphere. With the first ray of sun, I was out on the terrace to have a walk. It was then I got a little bit of relief. It is rightly said that fresh air and the early morning rising sun keep a man healthy, physically, and mentally.

After morning chores, I reached downstairs and sat down in the portico to go through the newspaper. Anil came to me and asked "Did you not sleep properly at night? I heard some sound of a hoarse throat almost all through the night."

This question from Anil made me burst into a deep cry and this panicked Anil who yelled "Abha, come soon. See what has happened to him."

Bhabhi came and consoled me "Do not cry, we understand your grief. Control yourself."

After a few minutes, I could hold my emotions.

Bhabhi asked, "From today onwards, you will sleep in my bedroom with your brother."

As last night's trauma had simply made me so jittery that I could not say no to Bhabhi despite knowing that my sleeping with Anil meant Bhabhi had to sleep separately.

I slept with Anil for two days and could sleep properly but then my conscience pricked me. I thought that just for my sake, I had made the husband and wife sleep separately. On the third day, I told Bhabhi that I would sleep in the drawing room. Though Bhabhi denied it, I put my foot down and started sleeping in the drawing room thereafter.

I left Kanpur on the 6th of September for Lucknow and attended the court on the 7th. Fortunately, the hearing was done that day and my deposition was completed after cross-examination by the advocate of the other party. On the 9th I flew back to Mumbai from Lucknow airport. My program was to go to Latur after the 20th but as Pankaj had tested COVID positive, the program was deferred.

In the meantime, I received an email from the corporate office of my bank informing me of my empanelment as Concurrent Auditor for the Lakhanpur branch, Kanpur. This was a welcome development. The faint idea of a Kanpur stay that had been simmering since I had a talk with Patnaik sir had started looking to happen. I was happy and worried as well. Happy because my feeble desire of staying in Kanpur had a support now and worried because it required separation from Kids and staying either with Anil or Gita or in my flat all alone. As an alternative, I also thought of living in an Ashram where others like me had been staying. I even contacted them over the phone. But neither Anil nor the kids permitted staying in the Ashram. The choice of everyone had been to stay with Anil, if I desired to stay in Kanpur. However, I comforted myself that I would take a call about staying at my flat or with Anil only after landing at Kanpur. Somehow, the sense of happiness had started outweighing the sense of worry. I had started thinking that it was an opportunity to test if I could stay in Kanpur alone and prove to myself that I was not wimp.

I sent my confirmation of acceptance of my assignment of Concurrent Auditor by mail followed by sending the required documents to the concerned offices through mail as well as by post. In the evening after sending the documents, I started thinking about my future vis a vis audit assignment. Somehow, I found my morale on a higher level.

Pankaj had recovered and I decided to leave Mumbai for Latur on the 3rd night and come back to Mumbai on the 9th morning, only to leave for Kanpur on the 10th. Air tickets and Rail tickets got booked.

As per plan I reached Latur on the 4th morning. I enjoyed my stay with little Bunny and visited a few places. I was scheduled to leave for Mumbai on the 8th night.

APNA DHYAN RAKHIYEGA

It was the night of 8th October 2021, I was at the station with Puja, Pankaj, and Bunny. I had to leave for Mumbai as on the 10th I had to go to Kanpur. Puja was extremely sad because this time I was going back to Kanpur to stay there on account of the audit assignment. She was quite worried about me and not sure whether I had what it takes to live alone. By now, I had almost decided to stay in my flat. Puja had been trying to avoid direct eye contact with me. I too was sad as I was going away from my kids to stay alone for the first time in my life.

The train started moving, I got shocks of grief as I was drifting away from my kids. Within seconds they stopped being visible. I gave a call to Puja, but she did not take it. I called again a few minutes later and it met the same fate.

Then a WhatsApp message from Puja flashed on my mobile reading "अपना ध्यान रखियेगा" (Take care of yourself). It was an emotional message vociferously speaking about Puja's state of mind and solicitude for me. Her next message read "Missing Mummy" Daughters are always close to parents and mine is no exception.

Now it was a time for role reversal. I sent messages to Puja in order to boost her morale. Puja as a young kid of less than 10 years had once boosted my sagging morale when I had been transferred to the Kamasin (Banda) branch of our Bank in June 1997. Her breaking down had made me a little weaker today. But I thought that sometimes people should be allowed to cry and vent out their feelings, so I had let Puja vent her feelings and cry.

"You cannot be strong all the Time,

Sometimes you just need to let your tears come out"

I spent a restless night on the train and reached Mumbai in the morning of 9th and Shivam's house by OLA taxi booked by Shivam. On the 10th I was booked to fly from Mumbai to Kanpur.

INHALE COURAGE.... EXHALE FEAR

I landed in Kanpur in the afternoon of 10th October for the start of the Concurrent Audit of our Lakhanpur branch from 11th. I had tutored myself hard during the flight that it was the high time I searched for happiness within myself by living all alone. I had been reiterating within myself that it was an opportunity to feed my faith and starve the fear inside me that had been haunting me every moment since Reena's passing away, making life miserable. A sense of self confidence had started germinating within me but still it was an "Easier-Thought-Than-Done" like situation in the face of the fear in the extreme within me. It was a herculean task to do. However, my determination had held my nerves and did not let me run away. I had started promising to myself during the flight that I would overcome all my fears, if not today but certainly someday, for sure. I just had to take the first step in this direction that could make it happen.

"A thousand-mile journey starts with a single first step."

The Himalayan question was how to make it happen. I felt like a Broken – Winged bird which was unable to fly. But there was no other option but to fly. Some thoughts about unknown fears had been holding my wings.

"There is nothing in this world that can trouble you more than your Thoughts"

But as we know what we want is always on the other side of our fear and until and unless we transcend that mountain of fear, we are not going to have a pleasant view.

At the Kanpur Airport, Laxman, Gita's driver had come to receive me. I reached Anil's place. As these were Nav Ratri days, I had asked both Bhabhi and Gita to purchase clothes for Maa Durga as Reena would do during Nav Ratri. Both Gita and Bhabhi had purchased the clothes but Bhabhi, for reasons known to her, expressed her inability to come along with me to my flat. I came to Gita's place with Laxman. Gita and Jijaji Came down to my flat. The temple was cleaned and Maa Durga was draped in new clothes. An hour thereafter, we left the flat. Laxman dropped Jijaji and Gita at their residence and me at Anil's. The next day, i.e., on 11th of October, I came to Lakhanpur branch for the start of the audit and went back to Anil's home in the evening.

Before I could turn weak again and my determination gave in, I sat down with Anil and Bhabhi and while discussing over a cup of tea, advised them "I have taken a call to stay at my flat."

"What! But with whom?" They were taken aback as they had never expected this decision from me. They were of the view that I would conduct the audit by staying at their place.

I told them "None, I will stay alone. Since Reena's demise, I have stayed with you, Shivam, Puja, Sheebu, Shilpi, Patnaik sir, Reeshu, Guddoo and even travelled to Golden Temple and Himachal but neither I got over the trauma nor found peace of mind. I had simply been running away from my fears instead of facing them thereby letting it have the snowball effect. I have been thriving only but not living. Inhaling and exhaling breath alone cannot be a measure of living a wholesome life. Until and unless I do what I fear the most, the fear will not leave me."

I further stated "I often ask myself as to why I have been running here and there despite having my own flat and every time I receive an answer from my inner self that it is because Reena is no more. And, this answer makes me miss Reena more."

I had not stopped putting up my case "Until and unless I start staying at my place this question would always pop up and disturb me. So, it is high time I turned tough and faced a tough situation by staying alone at my flat facing my fear head on."

"But you have never lived alone and even got broken on transfers, so it may be difficult for you to stay there all by yourself." Anil spoke.

"Well, ewe advise you to stay here and conduct the audit by living here. We are afraid you might fall sick if you stay there alone." Anil further tried to convince me.

"Of course, it is difficult. Rather it appears impossible but impossible itself says 'I M POSSIBLE.' Yes, living alone in the face of the present circumstances is the hardest task, but it might make me stronger. So let me go. If at all, I feel panicky at night, I would go downstairs and chat with the Guards of the society who remain awake throughout the night." I put my case strongly.

"The hardest walk is walking alone, but it is also, the walk that makes you the strongest."

Both Anil and Bhabhi were speechless and looked at each other. But they could see a fire in me to fight the tough life in a tougher manner. They unwillingly decided to let me go with a heavy heart and instructions "Whenever you felt low, you must not fight shy to call us or call on us."

On the 12th morning, I left Anil's place with my belongings and their blessings. All eyes were welled up. I was feeling extremely low and unaware of what the future had in store for me but, of course, with some amount of courage as well. In the evening I reached my flat.

My heart was wrenching as it was going to be my maiden visit to my flat not only without Reena but also without anyone. I reached the entrance of the flat with my bag. My hands were trembling, and I was in awe as how to open the door. But I had a bit of consolation as well because a man named Ramu, known to Gita, had to come to stay with me for an initial couple of nights.

With shaky hands, I took out the key and opened the lock. It was pitch dark inside exactly like the darkness within me. I switched on all the lights one by one. The FM radio and TV were put on play mode to create a semblance of some people being around. The photos of Pitaji and Amma were silently placed on the side rack of the gallery whereas Reena's was placed in the cabinet hung on the wall. I wondered how destiny had played with me as this cabinet was got made by Reena for placing the photos of Pitaji and Amma but instead of them, her photo had been placed over there.

I stared into the eyes of Pitaji and Amma and touched the photos with reverence and sought for their blessings. The photos appeared to be consoling me "परेशान ना हो बेटा। रीना हमारे पास पहुंच गई है और हमारे संरक्षण में सुरक्षित है। इसलिए दुखी न हो।" (Do not get perturbed Beta. Reena had reached us and is utterly safe under our loving care. So do not be so sad)

I kept on gazing at the photos of Pitaji and Amma and wished if only they were around; I might have cried under their comforting embrace.

I then came near Reena's photo and tears started rolling down. The wreath around Reema's photo almost brought me down. It was placed on her photo on Tehranvi. A mere glance at her photo with a wreath was a sentimental moment. I wished her all peace and sought for her spiritual support. While fetching myself a glass of water, I recaptured when I would be back from the office, a glass of water would always be waiting for me on the dining table. Every nook and corner appeared to be vouching for Reena's presence around.

While entering the Bedroom, my eyes got fixed to a photo hung on the wall featuring me, Reena, Pankaj, Puja, Shivam, and little Bunny. It was a selfie clicked by me at Hyderabad airport after Bunny's Mundan. A flashback of events just traversed through my eyes and tears started rolling. I thought how sublime the days were when we all were together.

As the time was passing by, I had been getting more emotional. It appeared my efforts to live alone would dissipate and I would have to either flock back to Anil and do the audit work from there or quit the audit and go back to Mumbai / Latur and stay with kids.

Ramu had reached by now. I looked at Ramu and thought how unpredictable life was as I had to piggyback on someone unknown to stay afloat in my own flat.

After dinner, feeling a little uneasy and low, I went downstairs and had a couple of rounds of my society. Walking around society has always been a stress buster for me.

After half an hour, I came back upstairs and watched TV and by 12 AM I retired. Ramu had been lying beside me where Reena used to lay. It gave me a sense of anger. I even thought of asking Ramu to sleep elsewhere as it was Reena's place to sleep. All the turbulence in my mind had kept sleep miles away. I kept on thinking if this was life why do we all get attached to anybody then? I remembered the talks I had with Reena during our honeymoon in 1986 when while walking around in Connaught Place, New Delhi, I had told Reena that we must not get attached to each other too much lest it might give excruciating pain in case of sudden separation for any reason. I thought about how life tests us. I had given Reena that advice but I myself had failed to follow that and now feel the pain of Reena's separation beyond measure. Somehow, sleep played its role and I slept, though late.

The maid had come and I did the morning chores. While having morning tea I travelled down memory lane and remembered how in the two specific coffee cups, I and Rena would have our morning tea together. I had a glance over those two coffee cups, with wet eyes, kept securely by me now in the crockery shelf as a token of that remembrance. After having breakfast, I started for the office and Ramu went off only to return in the night again. After two nights, I got a call from Capt. Rajiv, my old Bank friend. He asked me if I would like to visit Maa Pitambara Siddhapeeth in MP. I agreed and the next day we along with Vandana, his wife, visited there to have Maa's Darshan and sought for her blessings to enrich me with strength to tide over the present tough scenario.

The next day Gita called me and said "Ramu will come again today."

I politely refused and said "Gita, it is the high time I moved ahead all by myself with no crutches in the shape of human support or otherwise. It is my fight and I must fight it out alone. I need to escape from escapism and face the ground reality."

I continued "Gita if I remain dependent on someone, I will simply thrive but not live. So, for living a life gracefully, I need to brave the odds." Gita sounded worried over the phone and said "Ok, but take care. Anytime, you may call on us. Moreover, we are just a call away and we will be there for you always."

Hereafter, my solo fight against life started. I did not know which hidden power had kept me gathered. I realised that Reena's memories that would sink and haunt me earlier, had now started giving me strength. At night, I had started keeping Reena's photo beside me on the next pillow properly wrapped to keep her insulated from the cold. I would kiss her photo, bring it close to my heart to make her listen to my heartbeats and bring it close to my ear to let me hear her heartbeats. Though her heartbeat could not be heard literally, I always heard it virtually beating for me. I still do this before retiring and feel her presence. Besides, while going to the office, I kiss her photo and keep it on the pillow asking her to take care of the house as earlier till I return from the office. I am sure that Reena's virtual presence is the only strength that has kept me going then and now as well.

Though I had remained a regular visitor to my closest ones in town, it has been enigmatic why they, notwithstanding their always standing by me whenever I needed them and whom I had always thought to be the last resort to fall back on, did not consider it appropriate, after I had come to my flat to live alone, to call me or call on me at regular or even irregular intervals to make me feel I was not alone in this fight of survival. They could not envisage the pain I had been undergoing. On the other side, I thank my friends like Dixit ji, Chaturvedi ji, Shrawan ji, Salil, D.D. Gupta, Capt. Rajiv, Jaiprakash, Rajnish, Issac, Ankur, Ish, Ayushi, Ashish, Rajesh, Jitendra, Vinai, Shrikant, Subhash Mehrotra, Pramod, Darvesh, Sandeep etc. who really stood by me and kept calling me. A few of them had also been regular visitors to my place.

Vandana Pandey, my college mate, and Neera Handa, my earlier neighbour and RBI colleague, also stood by me and supported me by motivating me over phone calls. Hemant's daughter Shruti, son Anant and son-in-law Neeraj did their best to make me feel cared for by regular visits. Even Deepika, who had turned once in while caller for the last few years, had started taking my care by occasional but motivational calls and showing her concern for me. My ex-boss Patnaik Sir and Soma Bhabhi were always there for me and never let me feel alone by making video calls almost on a weekly basis. Their every call always had something that helped me get over the trauma. My fellow society residents too supported me in my worst days and always boosted my morale. It is true that when God fails to create blood relation with someone, he brings him or her as a friend to correct his mistake.

Gradually over a period, I had become a little bolder and started reducing the intake of anti-anxiety and sleeping pills, I had been taking for the last few months

Though I had been living one day at a time and not completely out of the vicious cycle of trauma, I continued with courage thinking… "ये वक्त गुजर जाएगा" (This time must pass), of course with Reena's virtual presence

MAIN HOON NA....

Just a few days after my solo stay in my flat, I watched Sanjai Dutt starrer old classic movie "Vastav", two scenes thereof had a moving effect on me. These were as narrated below…

SCENE 1: Mohinish Bahal, playing the role of Dutt's elder brother, says to his father that he has been allotted a flat by his employer and he wants to shift there with his wife. He further says that he is leaving the house only and not severing relations with the family. Going ahead he says that he will continue to send money every month to the family. His wife objects to his plan whereas his father looks bewildered and worried.

SCENE 2:. The camera now focuses on Dutt's mother, played by Reema Lagoo who looks at her harried husband and Dutt's father... and intervenes...

" तुम क्यों परेशान होते हो...मैं हूं ना..." (Why do you worry. I am here.)

Though the entire film was quite intense having jaw dropping scenes keeping not only me but the entire audience glued to the seats, these two scenes had just gone through my heart and made me compare my position with that of Dutt's parents in the film as my closest ones had turned indifferent towards me after I had shifted to my flat making me fend for myself and sail through turbulent waters all alone. Such attitude of theirs often made me revisit the dialogue of Reema Lagoo and I always wished in pain if only there was one to console me and say " तुम क्यों परेशान होते हो...मैं हूं ना..."

FESTIVALS SANS REENA

The Karwa Chauth, a festival when wives keep fast for the long lives of their husbands, was to be celebrated a few days after I had come to my flat. On this day, all officials of the office would leave office comparatively early to be with their wives. We would often cut jokes with one another to reach home early else we would be "Worshiped" first before actual worship. I too was no exception and would always reach home early.

As it was my first Karwa Chauth after Reena's passing away, Bhabhi had asked me to come over to their place. Gita too called from Delhi and suggested going to Anil. But I believed that Reena still lived in the flat and my staying put at Bhabhi's place on this day would mean leaving Reena alone and disrespecting her "Fast." I politely advised Bhabhi to let me celebrate with "Virtual Reena" and she could understand my sentiments. I reached home from the office. Like every year, the terraces of both the Towers of our society had been illuminated and opened for ladies to see the moon and break their fasts after doing puja and other rituals.

Every year I too would go upstairs with Reena where she would see the moon and after doing her puja would come back. Then I would drench her hair with water and give her some water to drink as well. This way her fast would get broken

This time in absence of Reena, I had to celebrate it all alone. I went to the terrace with Reena's photo on which I had pasted a "Bindi" (a coloured sticker pasted by Indian wives on their foreheads). I held the photo towards the moon and asked Reena's photo with teary eyes "Reena, the moon is here. Look at it and then break your fast. You have been without water and food since morning."

I requested one of my society members, Dr Bhagoliwal "Please take a snap along with the photo of Reena in my hand." Watching me celebrating the festival with Reena's photo, many members of my society had tears in their eyes. I saw a few ladies hiding their tears from me lest I should get weak.

I then came down for dinner with Reena's photo. My next-door neighbour, Savitri Bhabhi, had brought some specially made dishes for me. I put a few drops of water on Reena's lips followed by some eatables including a bit of sweets to break her fast. Thus, I could celebrate the Karwa Chauth literally without but virtually with Reena having tears in my eyes but pride in my heart. Though this all might seem dramatic to many, it was very soothing to me.

After ten days the biggest Indian festival Diwali was to fall. In our country, it is a tradition to buy wreaths during Diwali for the Photos of the close ones of the family who have passed away. Since our marriage, Reena would bring wreath for Pitaji and after Amma's demise, for her also. It was for the first time that I had to bring wreaths. But I had to buy not two but three, that extra one for Reena. It was too sentimental and unsettling moment to purchase three wreaths. But that is life and it often turns too hard making us its puppets. On Diwali day, I went to Anil with a packet of sweets, a tradition in north India. I had lunch there and stayed till evening and then sought for their permission to leave for my home. Both Anil and Bhabhi asked me to stay back at their residence and celebrate together. Though in the heart of my heart, I too wanted to stay there at night, the mere thought of Reena being alone in the flat did not let me stay there. I requested them to allow me to go. They could read my heart and allowed me to go but said "Ok, but come back after performing puja and lighting "Diyas." As my concern for Reena prevailed upon me, I convinced them to let me go and stay at my flat. Both saw confidence and love for Reena in my eyes and with a heavy heart allowed me to go.

I reached home at dusk. My maid helped me do the initial preparations. She cleaned the temple. Get the diyas ready with oil and wick in a big steel plate. At Muhurat time puja was performed with her help and Diyas were put at proper places to illuminate the house. I gave sweets to Reena by pasting a bit of it on her lips. I lit one Phuljhadi just for the sake of it and then went downstairs to celebrate the festival with society members. I remained there till 11 PM and came back when one of my colleagues Shruti Pawagi and her husband Rajesh had called on me. They came with a packet of sweets. They left after half an hour. Soon after some of my society members thought it proper to visit me that made me feel I was still being cared for. I kept the lights of the flat on till quite late. It is said Goddess Laxmi visits on Diwali night. Thus, my first Diwali celebrations sans Reena were over on a sombre note.

However, I can attest that while celebrating Diwali all alone I could feel Reena's presence in every nook and corner of the flat.

This was the second saddest Diwali for me after that of 25th October, 1973, the day when Pitaji was cremated.

REENA'S BIRTHDAY AFTER DEMISE

Somewhere in the month of December 2021, I had a call from the district administration "Is it someone from the home of Sandhya ji?"

"Yes," I replied.

"May I know Who is speaking?" asked the caller.

"I am Arun Misra, her husband," I said.

"Well, you know the state government has decided to give Rs. 50 K to the kith and kin of those who died from COVID-19. For that, you need to provide some documents at the District Magistrate's office." Advised the caller.

"But my wife had turned COVID-19 negative before she passed away." I clarified to him.

"Ok, but she was admitted to the hospital because of COVID 19 and she expired because of its attendant complications. So, fill in the form otherwise, you know, people here would manipulate and lodge fake claims on bogus identity and take payment." The caller emphasized.

"Ok, I will submit it tomorrow," I replied and thought it was better to lodge the claim and do some charity with the amount.

I lodged the claim the next day and I got an amount of Rs. 50 K credited to my account in 15 days. I sent Rs. 10 K each to Puja and Shivam with instructions to use the money, only for charity, the way they want. Puja used this in distributing Blankets and shawls to needy persons. Shivam got surgery done on one cat and arranged food for animals. I distributed dozens of blankets, and jackets and kept the remaining amount to be used for further charity as and when needed.

Going ahead, it was a coincidence that my closest friend, Hemant Dubey, shared his birthday with Reena on 23rd February. And, it is also no less than a coincidence that on, 22nd April, when Hemant left for his heavenly abode, Reena was admitted to hospital after saying those shocking words "देखो चल तो रहीं हूं पर लौट के नही आऊंगी."

In the meantime, Shruti, daughter of Hemant expressed her desire "Chacha how will it be to celebrate the birthdays of Papa and Chachi (Shruti addressed Reena as Chachi) together." Her offer was catchy and sentimental. I immediately consented. She wanted the birthdays to be celebrated with physically challenged kids. I thought it was time to use the funds received from the district administration. I zeroed in on a school of Visually challenged kids in Nehru Nagar, Kanpur.

I discussed it with the school authorities. They looked too happy to let us celebrate the birthdays in the school. I inquired if the school wanted something for blind kids. I was advised to support the school in purchasing Braille Books for kids. Later, the school preferred to go for customized walking sticks for the kids. I told the authorities to place the order for the same and I would pay on the day of the celebration. They had 80 kids in school and due to COVID-19, only 50 were present. It was a Boarding School.

On 23rd February, Shruti along with her Dadi, Mummy, Niraj, Anant, and others reached the school with two cakes, one for her Papa and one for Reena, as well as eatables and caps for the kids. I was alone from my side. The birthdays were celebrated by the kids with all enjoyment.

The celebration with Visually challenged kids gave me an awakening that if you move ahead in life keeping your limitations and challenges at bay, there is no stopping you and life could be wholesome notwithstanding all adversities, handicaps, and setbacks. On my query about how they felt being unable to see anything, none expressed dismay. Those who had lost eyesight after initial normal days said they did feel depressed initially but got used to it later. They had accepted the reality and did not feel challenged now. They were walking and talking to one another like normal kids and each of them was well-behaved, full of etiquette and did not forget to say "Thank you" whenever anything was given to them. The overall scenario had brought tears in my eyes and I saw Shruti sobbing in a corner as well.

The bravery of these visually challenged kids had given a boost to my morale and a lesson on how to move on notwithstanding difficulties staring in our faces. The kids had made me discern that Death means leaving Temporary Home for going to the Permanent Home. I had understood that both Reena and Hemant had left their Temporary Homes and gone to their Permanent Homes leaving their spiritual and virtual presence here.

Later, we thanked the School Authorities for letting us celebrate the birthdays of our departed dear ones with the brave kids. I paid cash to the centre in charge for their purchase of sticks for students. I along with Shruti, Niraj, Anant, their Dadi, Mummy, and others came out of the school mulling that not only these kids had braved their bigger challenges but also enlightened us about the meaning the life.

May the Almighty God be on their side always. Amen...

Our Marriage Anniversary After Reena's Passing Away

The wedding Anniversary is an important day in the lives of husband and wife. They look forward to it with all excitement. Sans one of the spouses, the wedding anniversary loses its sheen and when one of the two has passed away, it becomes meaningless and the associated pain reaches its worst, turning the anniversary into a nightmare. The one who, unfortunately, is left behind cries within his/her heart when the day falls. And, if it happens to be the first one after one of the spouses has left for heavenly abode, it is simply calamitous and the pain and agony that the surviving spouse goes through are unfathomable. The words find themselves short to express it. An already melancholy heart sinks deeper into pain. On this day what he/she needs is the sympathy and support of close ones either through calls or their calling on him/her.

It was 12th March 2022. It happened to be our 36th Wedding Anniversary and the first after Reena's sad demise. It was the 2nd Saturday, a Bank holiday, and I was alone in the house feeling a lot gloomy. It was about 9 AM in the morning, I was sitting in my living room staring blankly and submerged in Reena's memories. A mere comparison between our first anniversary and the first anniversary after her death was simply unsettling. I also reminisced about our 25th anniversary celebrated with the kids in a hotel in Dehradun and the last one celebrated at Cawnpore club in the company of Jijaji, Gita, Anil, Bhabhi and Summi, Bhabhi's maid.

While deep into my pain and sitting on my sofa, I had been expecting calls from Gita and Anil, for their being my real elder sister and brother respectively. I also hoped that Anil would call on me or ask me to call on him. Gita and Jijaji were in Delhi, hence their calling on me was ruled out.

At about 11 AM my mobile started ringing. It was a call from Gita. She asked me sympathetically "Beta what should I say? I can neither say Happy anniversary nor ask you to forget Reena. I understand your pain. But nobody can do anything. You must live with it somehow. Beta, keep yourself happy as far as possible by being busy, though, I know, it is very difficult."

While talking to Gita, my efforts to hold back my emotions gave in and I started sobbing. Gita's voice looked sad too but she tried to assuage my emotions "Do not cry beta. Be strong. You better go to your friends or watch some movie. You can also think of going to Anil and Abha. It will help you mitigate your pain."

Gita's suggestion to go to friends or Anil made my latent frustration burst "Why should I go to Anil or for that matter anyone? Is it not the duty of Anil and Bhabhi to call me and ask me to come over there? Can they not visualise which mental state I am in?"

"Yes, it is their duty but they might be fighting shy to call you. I too was nervous in calling and wishing you when Reena is no more. I took time to muster the courage to call you. Your Jijaji is sitting beside me but failing to have the courage to talk to you. Beta as you are alone, so I would reiterate that it is advisable to go to Anil. Staying put at home all alone would hurt you more." Gita suggested.

This suggestion added fuel to the fire. I exploded in anger "Do you think I am so namby-pamby that I will go places to seek support or cry on their shoulders? I am sad and in tremendous pain, but not as effete as you think I am. I will not go to anyone.

If they do not call, it is ok. I will prefer crying in isolation to finding happiness on the crutches of someone. And, if at all they find it difficult to call, why cannot they, at least, call on me? Is it correct to leave someone close to you to cry in isolation missing his wife on such a day?"

I disconnected the phone and cried profusely only to be consoled by myself after a few minutes. After Reena's passing away, I had cried several times in isolation earlier also and only one person had always come to my rescue and helped me get gathered. And the person had been none other than myself.

I was contemplating if close relations like brothers could not come up to stand by us when we are at our lowest ebb then what use these relations were for? My entire day passed in crying, and consoling myself but I kept my fingers crossed and even waited for the call of Anil and Bhabhi till I retired at night. After all, both had been very supportive, particularly after the major car accident in 2016 and after the demise of Reena as well.

The indifferent attitude of Anil and Bhabhi had made me recollect that while purchasing the flat in Kanpur in 2018 after selling the one in Lucknow, purchased in 2001 out of a bank loan, notwithstanding Reena's preference to Lucknow over Kanpur, I had argued that Kanpur was better for us as I had my brother, sister, and other relatives besides friends to stand by me in case of need. Now I am afraid Reena would be turning in her grave on finding me crying in isolation, particularly on such a day.

Despite my outburst over the phone during the call with Gita, I tried to persuade myself that both Anil and Bhabhi might have forgotten my special day. And, forgetting one's anniversary or birthday is not a crime as, in past, not only Anil but I also had missed wishing each other on such days. But today's case was different for obvious reasons and my expectations were not exaggerated either. After all, when Gita was not in the city, who other than Anil and Bhabhi were there, I could have fallen back on. My kids had offered to come to Kanpur but I had refused them as I had already booked my tickets to visit Mumbai three days after on 15th to celebrate Holi with Shivam scheduled on the 18th and then to Latur to stay with Pankaj, Puja, and my little Champ Bunny.

After passing my entire gloomy day, I was a bit gathered by the evening. I planned to celebrate my anniversary all alone thinking our anniversary was not a reminder that Reena had passed away, rather it was reminiscent of the fact that our bond of love had been eternal and vibrating even after her being no more physically. To feel a little euphoric, I took a couple of drinks. I had brought Rabri (a sweet dish made from milk) and cake. Thereafter, I arranged for dinner not on the dining table but on my bed by spreading a newspaper. I brought the photo of Reena and kissed it. Thereafter, I stuck a little bit of Rabri and cake on Reena's lips and wished her "Happy 36th Anniversary dear". I took noodles for dinner. As Reena had also been fond of noodles, I stuck a noodle too on her lips. While doing all this I looked deep into her photo and questioned "Where have you gone Rinnie, why did you not think how would I survive without you?"

Though my eyes were teary, the drinks played the role of mood booster and helped bust my emotional stress. I clicked a photo of the dinner plate with Reena's photo.

On the 13th I had to go to Anil's place to collect some Ghujhiyas (a sweetmeat prepared specially on Holi)) and Namkeen prepared by Bhabhi on the demand of Puja and Shivam. I had lunch at Anil's place and came back in the evening. During my stay at their place, I kept expecting that before I left their place, they would certainly convey belated anniversary wishes. Both talked about everything under the sun but for my marriage anniversary. This surprised me a lot but still I thought my anniversary date had slipped from their mind.

In the night, I took a couple of drinks again and then had my dinner. I thought of sending a message to Bhabhi reminding her to have forgotten my anniversary purely in a lighter vein without any malice. Accordingly, I sent a photo clicked on the anniversary night with Reena's photo, cake, my dinner plate, and a glass of alcohol with a message as under....

"Celebrated my 36th Anniversary yesterday with Reena. She ate Rabri n cake. I took these two besides drinks and noodles. Reena stays with me always and she never forgets to be with me, particularly at night. Wish me today as you and Anil both forgot to wish me yesterday and today also. "बड़े बड़े शहरों में ऐसी छोटी छोटी बातें होती रहती है" (such small things keep happening in big cities). Belated wishes are also welcome."

Unfortunately, my message was not taken in the right spirit by Bhabhi and Anil had to call me to lodge his protest the next morning. To date, I have failed to comprehend if, at all, there was anything offensive in my message. The humour-soaked language of the message speaks volumes of it being purely straight from the heart. I think, Bhabhi and Anil, instead of "Reading" the hidden emotions of this innocuous message through the "Heart." "Read" it with the "Mind". I am of the considered opinion that maintaining relations does not require too much application of "Mind" and "Brain". The "Heart" is enough to let the relationship flow smoothly.

I, now, curse myself why, at all, I sent a message to them in the first place.

On 9th May 2022 was Reena's first death anniversary. Invitations to all close relatives had been sent over the phone by Puja. I did not make any call to anyone in this regard. A Havan had to be done. A pandit ji had been invited. Puja, Pankaj, and Bunny had also come. Shivam could not come because of his professional commitment. After Havan meals were served to those present and sent to some flats of the building.

As I had already decided to do charity on the day of Reena's first anniversary, I electronically sent Rs.10 K to a school of Deaf & Dumb I had already zeroed in.

All close relatives were present barring Anil and Abha who were conspicuous by their absence. The questions were raised by a few among those present about their not being present. I was in a predicament about what to say as I had no answer.

FROM BEHIND TO AHEAD OF THE FEAR CURVE

The demise of a spouse is considered as one of the most calamitous losses one may suffer in one's life. The gravity and intensity of the pain associated with it and its persistence are directly proportional to the intensity of emotional bonding we had with the soulmate who has passed away. The pain we go through after death is the cost, we pay for the attachment we had with the departed soul. I would often feel angry with God why he cherry-picked Reena to undergo the suffering before she left for her ultimate destination and at other times cursed myself why I had been left behind to grieve. I was completely broken and unable to find a way to pick up the pieces to come back to my normal self. But sometimes, a small incident can be inspiring and life-changing....

After Reena's death, I was the least concerned about the upkeep of the house. Every evening, I would notice certain pieces of weeds always littering the 9th-floor balcony of my flat, and the next morning, I found none of the pieces. Later, I noticed that my maid had been sweeping all the weeds lying there in the discharge of her regular duties. One fine morning, after the maid had gone, I saw a little bird bringing small pieces of weeds and keeping them in a corner of the balcony. I could appreciate the weeds being swept off by the maid daily were the pieces brought by this little bird. The very next morning, I prevented my maid from sweeping off these pieces. Within a couple of days, a nest was ready and the bird started staying there. This made me realize a cliché but crucial lesson that if a tiny bird could re-build its nest, after it had been completely shattered several times, by bringing in many a motley piece from various sources regularly, why could I not reassemble the pieces of my confidence back to re-build the nest of self-belief within me to live a wholesome life?

However, the double whammy of loneliness and the thought that I would never see Reena again had been having its toll on me. The convergence of grief and loneliness was complicated. Though the desire had ignited within me to quit being sad and start smiling, loneliness always followed me like a shadow and had created a web of unknown fears inside me notwithstanding my efforts to convince myself that these internal and imaginary fears were bigger than the real ones outside. I was just overwhelmed by the stormy clouds of the past. The situation had become so fluid that I was unable to have control over my thoughts whereas the need to focus on taking hold of thoughts was immediately called for. There is no denying that at some stage of life, circumstances turn such as we must let go of the past and move on thinking when life gets tough, we cannot wish it to be easier, rather we need to resolve to be stronger. Of course, it is not an easy task and was not easy for me as well. Summoning all my invisible strengths was immediately warranted as it might help me finally let go the baggage of my past.

"Do not let hindsight hinder foresight,
let the past be in the past."

I knew if I remained a prisoner to the past, my promise to myself to overcome my fears would never see the light of day. It was the do-or-die moment. Going back to the kids or Anil would have meant surrendering before the odds meekly and coming back to square one with an egg on my face. But some inner power kept me gathered and going.

The latent meaning of Sadguru's preaching **"People who have truly, immensely loved each other are the ones who will handle the loss of the loved one gracefully"** had started making me discern that Reena had only gone from a physical to a spiritual world and our love had been and will remain stronger than death. I had started realising that just one part of her had been taken by death, the rest was still in me. After all, those who love us genuinely, never go away but rather walk along with us holding our hands.

***"Death is a comma, not a full stop,
it is a transition to another level of existence,
not the termination of existence."***

I had figured out that it was mandatory to accept Reena's death for moving on even though it was hard...to talk as much as I could ...and not to hold back my emotions. It is sometimes okay to show emotions and be weak. I had realized that the world still needed me, my breath still counted and I should live for Reena as well as on her behalf as it would make her and me happy.

I had understood that the quickest way of overcoming fear was to take fear head-on and do what I dreaded the most. But here was the mountain of fear and I was standing just below fearing to start scaling it. At this juncture, what was needed was to take the first baby step which looked the toughest.

***"The first step is hardest but once you take your
first baby step, things will get easier from then on"***

While fighting with myself and my fears, I made the first step bravely remembering the famous tagline of a soft drink... डर के आगे जीत है (victory lies beyond the fear)

And I did not know how, but it worked wonders for me. I was back on rails. I started playing with kids of the society and bartering chocolates for their innocent smiles. This somehow started making my evenings. One little kid named Daivik Gupta, who calls me Dadu, became my the most preferred kid in the society. His innocence motivated me to write my fate myself instead of letting life write my fate. I also started mingling with people of my age. I revived my passion for reading books. Last but not least, I started writing lyrics of songs as well as singing and recording them on my mobile, some emotional ones to vent out my inner pain and others to motivate myself. And, believe me this all facilitated my revitalization and regeneration.

I realized that this solo fight against odds and adversities of life had introduced me to myself and I could find something more important than fear and that was **"I & My life."** Now, Life had started looking it had got some purpose to move on. I had convinced myself that though kids, relatives and friends were mine, my own life was no less important.

Having sailed through the turbulent waters of the sea of life, I could perceive that though unpredictable…life is beautiful, though uncertain…life is surprising. And, living life with full conviction while wavering through bewilderment is an art. Every moment there are probabilities, possibilities, and certainties that somebody somewhere in this world might suffer from failure, the loss of a loved one, or a catastrophe. But what matters is that life teaches us how to handle the situation tactfully and deal with problems courageously as courage is nothing but the fear turned inside out. Such enlightenment had brought me on a positive track. The anti-anxiety and sleeping pills I had been taking for the last couple of months had started getting withdrawn gradually leading to a complete withdrawal.

However, there is no denying that life sans Reena still hurts. But this hurt is a gift of sorts. It reminds me of how much Reena's life meant to me...! How wonderful the 35-plus years of togetherness have been...! The hurt means how Reena brought love to me as my wife...! The hurt means how Reena became a mother as she joyously welcomed two sweet babies into this world and raised them in love...! The hurt means how as a friend and wife I could count on Reena for love and support...! I have realized that things will never be as normal as before but I also know there will be a new normal. I know that as much as I feel alone, I am not. Visiting kids or anyone is a pleasure trip now, not a trip for my survival and existence. The almighty God has been kind to me as Pankaj has been transferred to Mumbai and both of my kids are now based in Mumbai. My life now moves on with a philosophy that our physical existence on the earth is perishable whereas our soul is immortal.

I can, now, attest that my Loneliness has crossed boundaries and entered the territory of Solitude..., whose silence allows me to hear Reena's whispers..., whose every breeze carries Rena's fragrance...., whose heart beats in unison with Reena's heart.... Yes, I know she is not gone, rather lives on in my heart and walks alongside me, holding my hands.

"How can the dead be truly dead
when they still live in the souls
of those who are left behind"

Now, I do not mourn that our journey of togetherness has ended, rather, I smile with pride that it happened and we traversed it together. I have mastered the art of living alone by overcoming all my fears

Besides, I had started singing the songs written, composed, and sung by me with an air of confidence in myself and with an inkling of Reena being around. One of my such songs is as it goes….

जो हुआ सो हुआ अब न सोंचों क्या हुआ
जिंदगी के इस सफर में जो लड़ा सो जिया
कौन इस जहां में जिसने झेला न हो गम,
ज्यादा होता किसी का तो किसी का है ये कम,
गम के आगे झुका न वो सिकंदर हो गया
जो हुआ सो हुआ अब न सोचों क्या हुआ...
लगता था टूटकर हम बिखर जायेंगे,
तेरे बिन इस जहां में अब न जी पाएंगे
पर तभी तेरी यादों ने सहारा दे दिया
जो हुआ सो हुआ अब न सोंचो क्या हुआ...

Now, whenever in isolation and in absence of kids, who are away in Mumbai, I tend to feel low and ponder who is there to put a consoling hand on my shoulders, I virtually feel Reena comes calling, putting her hand on my shoulders, and whispering in my ears….

तुम क्यों परेशान होते हो...मैं हूं ना...

….. because I have risen like a phoenix and my promise to myself of overcoming someday has been fulfilled. Now, I proudly declare that I have come up trumps and traversed the traumatic path boldly ……

From behind the fear curve to ahead of the Fear Curve

Virtually holding Reena's hands with a conviction to hold her hands again literally up above in the heaven,

…coz that is what we truly deserve,

This piece of writing is my confession.

Note to the readers-

So, if you have lost someone, be patient with yourself. You do not need to understand everything at once, take one day at a time and do not mask your emotions, there is no shame in asking for help. And if you need support, reach out to your family, friends, myself, or helplines.